I-M-ABLE
Individualized Meaning-Centered Approach to Braille Literacy Education

Diane P. Wormsley

AFB PRESS
American Foundation for the Blind

I-M-ABLE: Individualized Meaning-Centered Approach to Braille Literacy Education, is copyright © 2016 by AFB Press, American Foundation for the Blind, 2 Penn Plaza, Suite 1102, New York, NY 10121. All rights reserved. No part of this work may be reproduced or transmitted in any form or by any means, electronic or mechanical, including photocopying and recording, or by any information storage or retrieval system, except as may be expressly permitted by the 1976 Copyright Act, or in writing from the publisher. Requests for permission should be addressed in writing to AFB Press, American Foundation for the Blind, 2 Penn Plaza, Suite 1102, New York, NY 10121.

Printed in the United States of America

Library of Congress Cataloging-in-Publication Data

Names: Wormsley, Diane P., 1946- author.
Title: I-M-ABLE : individualized meaning-centered approach to braille literacy education / Diane P. Wormsley.
Other titles: I'm able
Description: First Edition. | New York : AFB Press, American Foundation for the Blind, 2016. | Includes bibliographical references and index.
Identifiers: LCCN 2015039370 | ISBN 9780891287223 (pbk. : alk. paper) | ISBN 9780891287230 (epub) | ISBN 9780891287247 (mobi) | ISBN 9780891287254 (online subscription)
Subjects: LCSH: People with visual disabilities—Education.
Classification: LCC HV1626 .W76 2016 | DDC 371.91/146—dc 3
LC record available at http://lccn.loc.gov/2015039370

Developed with funding from the North Carolina Department of Public Instruction grant awards EP4814218 and NC10051133, provided in 2011–2012 and 2013.

The American Foundation for the Blind removes barriers, creates solutions, and expands possibilities so people with vision loss can achieve their full potential.

It is the policy of the American Foundation for the Blind to use in the first printing of its books acid-free paper that meets the ANSI Z39.48 Standard. The infinity symbol that appears above indicates that the paper in this printing meets that standard.

To my husband, Bill, the anthropologist, who has helped shape my understanding of cultural relevance and has thus helped shape this approach.

Contents

Acknowledgments   vii

CHAPTER 1   Introduction to I-M-ABLE   *1*

CHAPTER 2   Getting Started: Assessment and Incorporating Early Literacy Instruction   *10*

CHAPTER 3   Helping Students Select Key Vocabulary Words or Phrases   *35*

CHAPTER 4   Introducing Key Vocabulary Words and Phrases   *42*

CHAPTER 5   Teaching Students to Track across Multiple Lines of Braille   *69*

CHAPTER 6   Teaching Writing Mechanics in a Meaningful Way   *75*

CHAPTER 7   Collaborating with Students to Create Key Vocabulary Stories   *87*

CHAPTER 8   Using Key Vocabulary Words to Teach Phonics, Letter Recognition, and Contractions   *98*

CHAPTER 9   Applying and Expanding the Student's Reading and Writing Vocabulary   *111*

CHAPTER 10   Helping Students Read Fluently   *117*

References   123

Appendix   127

Resources   141

Index   149

About the Author   154

Acknowledgments

Many thanks to Julie Kagy of the North Carolina Department of Public Instruction for her belief in, and support of, I-M-ABLE.

Thanks to the project consultants whose contributions have made this a better practice guide and project: Dr. Frances Mary D'Andrea, Dr. Jane Erin, Dr. Penny Rosenblum, and Ms. Anna Swenson.

Special thanks to the North Carolina teachers who participated in the I-M-ABLE study in 2011–2012: Sherry Cataldo, Paula Justice, Jill McMillan, Susan Shepard, Norma Sirkisoon, Kerri Smith, Susan Smith, Brenda Stevens, Mirella Timms, and Annette Vinding. And very special thanks to all of their wonderful students!

Special thanks to Ms. Victoria Poole; and to Molly Myers and Rachel Popov, graduate assistants, 2011–2012; and Chelsea Privette, graduate assistant, 2012–2014.

CHAPTER 1

Introduction to I-M-ABLE

I-M-ABLE was first introduced to the world in the publication *Braille Literacy: A Functional Approach* (Wormsley, 2004). The book described an approach for teaching braille literacy that differed from the traditional approaches being used with braille readers in most school districts. It was derived from a whole-word approach described by Sylvia Ashton-Warner in her book *Teacher* (1963). Ashton-Warner, who taught Maori children in New Zealand, began reading instruction with words that she called *key vocabulary words*—words that had strong emotional meaning and appeal for her students—rather than beginning with letters or even words that did not hold as great an emotional appeal.

Braille Literacy: A Functional Approach was a first attempt to describe how Ashton-Warner's approach could be adapted for braille reading for several groups of at-risk learners who could benefit from the meaning-centered approach. The at-risk learners included students of all ages with visual impairments who had additional disabilities, from mild to severe, including those who were deaf-blind and those who were not making progress in learning to read braille. It also included late elementary up to high school–age students who were switching from print to braille, students who were learning English as a second language, and adults who had recently lost vision and who could no longer read print efficiently.

In the ten plus years since *Braille Literacy* was published, I have watched as teachers implemented this approach with a variety of school-age students with additional disabilities. It soon became obvious that the approach needed a different name. The term "functional" too often had teachers thinking that the words that should be used for beginning instruction were to be taken from daily living skills activities and that these would be the thrust of the literacy activities taking place within the context of the approach as well. In an attempt to rectify that misunderstanding, I renamed the approach I-M-ABLE: Individualized Meaning-Centered Approach to Braille Literacy Education. This name comes from a different assumption about the learners with whom teachers are using the approach: that they are able to learn to read.

Just as it became obvious that a new name was needed, it also became obvious from teachers' questions and concerns that they needed more direction on how to implement each of the various components of the approach. This need was the impetus for creating this practice guide for implementing I-M-ABLE. The intention is that teachers working with children who are visually impaired will use this handbook to guide them in implementing the approach, and that the same guide would be available for personnel preparation programs to use in coursework for preservice teachers learning how to teach braille reading. This practice guide is meant to be a resource for teachers to turn to when encountering a student who has extreme difficulty learning using traditional reading approaches.

The target population considered in this guide for I-M-ABLE consists of students who are candidates for braille reading but who have not made progress in learning to read, or whom teachers feel will have difficulty making progress because they have additional mild to moderate cognitive impairments. While the approach can be useful for students with other types of conditions such as English language learners, or children who have a hearing impairment or autism, or those with more severe cognitive disabilities, the present handbook does not address those students' needs directly.

DECIDING TO USE A DIFFERENT APPROACH

If you are reading this practice guide, very likely you have a braille student who has not been successful in learning to read braille, or you haven't found an appropriate approach for a particular student and are looking for something different. You are not alone, for approximately 60 percent of the population of children who are blind or visually impaired have additional disabilities (Bishop, 1991; Ferrell, Shaw, & Dietz, 1998), which make it difficult if not impossible for them to learn in a traditional manner.

I-M-ABLE differs from traditional approaches to teaching reading in several ways. The bulleted points below are described in depth throughout the various chapters of this handbook:

- Formal reading instruction begins with words or phrases rather than letters as a base.
- Instruction is individualized and centered around what is meaningful to students, drawing on their own backgrounds and experiences.

- Lessons are student-centered and student-driven.
- Teaching and learning are designed to accommodate gaps in students' experiential backgrounds, including gaps in early literacy instruction and experiences.
- Student engagement and motivation to learn to read and write braille are fostered in every lesson.
- Diagnostic teaching is incorporated into every lesson.
- Training in proper hand and finger usage in reading braille using motivating and meaningful tracking materials is incorporated into reading from the beginning of instruction.
- Decoding (phonics) instruction uses a whole-to-part phonics approach starting with words that students already are familiar with (Moustafa, 1997) and then extending to unfamiliar words.
- Comprehension is addressed by beginning with vocabulary that is meaningful to students and then adding to that base to expand the students' vocabulary and knowledge of the world.
- Fluency building is incorporated into lessons once students have a large enough reading vocabulary to begin reading sentences and stories.

For those who are interested in seeing how each of these components is supported by research, a comprehensive rationale for using this approach can be found in Wormsley (2011).

BEING RESPONSIVE TO STUDENTS

I-M-ABLE is different for every student with whom it is used because each student brings a different background and set of experiences to the school setting. Students who have been struggling to learn to read using traditional approaches need reading instruction that is tailored to their experiences and is as meaningful to them as possible. To accomplish this, teachers need to begin by getting to know these students well.

Many times students who have been unable to learn to read are not thought of as capable of reading by teachers or even their peers. Being responsive to students means accepting them for who they are and asking them to demonstrate the things they value (Kliewer, 2008). All students have likes and dislikes, things they enjoy doing and things they don't, and they are capable of expressing these preferences if teachers pay attention. Being responsive to students means showing respect for the things the students like and dislike without imposing value judgments on them. One student's favorite activities and possessions may be totally different from another's. One student may thoroughly enjoy playing with a tactile ball that has a bell in it; another may be obsessed with shows like *American Idol* or *The Voice* and their latest contestants. Using the same list of vocabulary words for every student does not acknowledge those individual differences; a teacher who is being responsive to students will understand that a student's word lists will be individualized according to the interests of that student. Paying attention to a student's distinct interests permits the teacher to recognize each child's individuality and utilize that to help the child develop literacy.

Teachers who are responsive to students learn from their students in ways they might not anticipate. One teacher who used this approach had never heard of the singer Lady Gaga until her student asked for Lady Gaga as a new key vocabulary word. After researching Lady Gaga to assure herself that the singer really did exist and to learn how to spell her name, the teacher began listening to Lady Gaga's music and discovered that she liked it. As she began playing the music, she and her student also began to have conversations about Lady Gaga and the songs she sang. By showing an interest in something that was important to her student, the teacher connected with her student in a way that showed respect for the student's choices in music. This in turn increased the student's sense of self-worth as she realized that she had something of value to contribute to their teacher/student partnership.

IMPORTANCE OF USING STUDENTS' BACKGROUNDS OF EXPERIENCE (SCHEMA)

> What we bring to the reading process determines what we take away *(Anderson, Hiebert, Scott, & Wilkinson, 1985).*

When reading a book, each of us interprets what we read based on our own *schema*, or background experience, and the content of the material we are reading. Having the appropriate schema helps in decoding words, understanding what we are reading, and reading fluently. Knowing a student's background and experiences enables teachers to help a student relate that previous knowledge to what is currently being learned. This in turn facilitates the learning of new ideas and concepts. The teacher can also ensure that the student is applying the appropriate schema to help interpret what is being read.

For example, in a story about Halloween that a teacher was reading aloud to a group of students who were visually impaired, there was a passage about a shadow that frightened the story characters. The teacher asked the students what a shadow was. Most students didn't answer. The one student who did answer talked about a character known as "The Shadow" with whom students were familiar from a current television show. By recognizing that students simply didn't have experience with the typical sense of the word *shadow* as it was used in the story, the teacher was able to provide a lesson the next day demonstrating this other meaning of shadow and explaining how it might be frightening. Once the students grasped the concept of a shadow, she read the story to them again. This time the students demonstrated a better understanding of the story and why the children in the story were afraid of the shadow.

Helping students apply past experiences to what they are learning permits students to better comprehend what they are reading. Chapters 2 and 3 provide suggestions for assessing students and finding out about their backgrounds and experiences and what is most meaningful to them.

IMPORTANCE OF DIAGNOSTIC TEACHING

Diagnostic teaching is "the process of continuously trying a variety of instructional strategies and materials based on the current needs of the students" (Opitz, Rubin, & Erekson, 2011, p. 23). I-M-ABLE is a diagnostic teaching approach in which instruction is centered on continuously analyzing the strengths and needs of students, placing particular emphasis on meaningful instruction based on prior experiences. I-M-ABLE teachers are flexible, constantly seeking and using student feedback and progress to determine what to include in lessons as well as how to vary the pace of lessons. I-M-ABLE teachers are willing to set aside a planned lesson to respond to what students are engaged in. They recognize and take advantage of "teachable moments." This student-centered instruction helps maintain students' engagement and motivation and focuses on what they can do, rather than perpetuating their struggle to learn.

While this I-M-ABLE practice guide is organized by components of the approach, there is no fixed order to how the various components are introduced or used on a daily basis other than the initial activities needed in order to get started and introduce key vocabulary words. So much of this approach depends on being respectful and responsive to students and what is important to them. It also depends on the teacher's ability to determine what each child is capable of at any given point in the process of learning to read.

GUIDING PRINCIPLES OF I-M-ABLE

What is important to remember throughout the use of the approach is that I-M-ABLE is built on four important principles, shown in Figure 1.1: motivation, engagement, individualization, and success. These four principles form the basis of everything we do in I-M-ABLE, as explained in the following sections.

Motivation

Those who work with children who are struggling readers talk a lot about how to motivate them. Children who are good readers don't need to be motivated to read. They have discovered what struggling readers aren't able to discover—that reading is its own reward. Reading a book can provide excitement that equals that of winning a video game or watching a good television show or movie. But if a child can't read well, he or she isn't able to experience the rewards that reading can bring. The challenge facing teachers is motivating struggling readers to develop into readers who can experience the benefits of such rewards.

Engagement

The key to motivation is engagement. Reading has to be something that involves the learner. The words and stories a student is learning to read need to be something so interesting that the child is immediately motivated to read that word or story.

Individualization

The key to engagement is individualization, or personalization, and this is the core of I-M-ABLE. What motivates me may not motivate you. If teachers wish to engage students in reading, they need to get to know them—what their interests

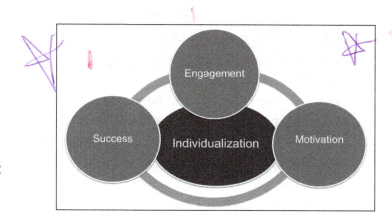

FIGURE 1.1

Guiding Principles of I-M-ABLE

are, what "turns them on." In I-M-ABLE, that is where reading instruction begins. If struggling readers can be motivated and engaged by carefully crafting reading instruction that relates to what engages those readers, then more than half the battle has been won in helping overcome reading difficulties.

4. Success

Just as most adults do not enjoy failure, children don't enjoy learning when they are not succeeding. Children who are blind and have additional cognitive disabilities may already have a history of failure in learning to read, and for them the reading experience may not be enjoyable. While creating a program that engages and motivates them is important, it is equally important that these children experience success when learning to read and write. In order to assure success in reading, I-M-ABLE teachers don't ask students to show how they can do something until it is certain they can do it. The time to test students in this approach is when teachers know they can pass the test! Students aren't asked to tell teachers what a word or phrase is until it has been taught to them so completely that they are absolutely accurate in reading the word or phrase.

Teachers should take care to place students in situations where they are able to do the tasks asked of them. For instance, one way to motivate and engage children in reading is to play games with words. However, if the child doesn't know how to play, the game will not be very much fun. Obviously, identification of the words used is a prerequisite to playing games with those words, especially if the child is to be successful in playing the game. But it is also important to build up the knowledge of the rules of the game. In a matching game, for example, teachers can use task analysis to isolate the various game steps and build practice in locating the cards for the game and matching them. Starting with a few cards for the game and then adding more as the student demonstrates capability in locating and matching cards will help the student learn to be successful. With building success in mind, a teacher can still be flexible and permit the child to direct the lessons as long as the result is not frustrating for the child.

HOW TO USE THIS PRACTICE GUIDE

Each of the chapters in this practice guide deals with one component of the I-M-ABLE approach and provides suggestions for how to introduce it. It is recommended that teachers not familiar with the approach read each chapter and implement the suggestions in that chapter with a student before moving on to another chapter. Once a student demonstrates some initial success, the teacher can expand on that success by incorporating elements of the learned component into any following lesson to which the component applies. Record keeping is obviously important. The Appendix provides copies of the various forms used in the component chapters. Once each of the chapters has been read, teachers can incorporate a variety of strategies on a daily basis.

While the approach begins with whole words and continues whole-word instruction for a considerable period of time until students have a fairly large reading vocabulary, phonics instruction is also an important component of the approach. Wormsley and McCarthy (2013) found that students who tended to have more success were those whose teachers were able to incorporate activities involving phonics and word-building skills into their lessons. The most important thing to remember is that assuring students' success with all of the various activities will help the student stay motivated. Allowing the student to be a "director" of his or her own learning will help maintain the student's engagement.

The components of the I-M-ABLE approach, described in detail in this practice guide, include the following:

- Getting started and incorporating early literacy instruction.
- Helping students select key vocabulary words and phrases.
- Introducing key vocabulary word or phrase cards.
- Teaching efficient use of the hands in reading through tracking across multiple lines of braille.
- Teaching writing mechanics in a meaningful way and utilizing technology tools.
- Collaborating with students to select and create stories for reading.
- Teaching phonics, letter recognition, and contractions using key vocabulary and filler words.
- Applying and expanding the student's reading and writing vocabulary.
- Building fluency in reading.

Deciding to use I-M-ABLE with students is the beginning of an incredible journey. To provide an idea of what lies ahead, here are some comments from a teacher who used this approach with her student, Hannah, and wrote each week about how Hannah was taking to this new approach to reading and writing braille:

> Hannah's new words were *love*, which she didn't seem to have any trouble with—luckily the brailled *love* key ring came at the right time to reinforce it! The other word was *Doll Kimmy*, which is a doll that has been loved by Hannah since she was a baby (and shows it).

Michelle (Hannah's mother) has also had time to check out some sites on the Internet and has decided that braille merchandise will be the gift she gives to her friends and family (as well as Hannah) this year. Hannah is very lucky to have such an involved mom.

Hannah is progressing so much faster than I thought possible—feels a bit like a roller coaster right now and I'm not good with speed! . . . She is having so much fun at the moment and I am discovering a sense of humor that I didn't know existed. I would never have predicted her as a girl who would choose *naughty* and *poo* as some of her earliest words! She is getting heaps of positive comments from everyone.

The next chapter presents the starting blocks for this approach, and also provides information about early literacy activities to include to make sure students aren't missing out on any of those essential elements of literacy.

CHAPTER 2

Getting Started: Assessment and Incorporating Early Literacy Instruction

Chapter 1 introduced the rationale behind the I-M-ABLE approach and the types of students for whom this approach might be helpful. These are students who are not yet readers, who are struggling to learn to read or may even have determined that they don't want to learn, and who are still in the beginning stages of literacy development. Typically developing children go through various stages as part of learning to read. These stages are described in Table 2.1.

Children who are visually impaired with additional disabilities may not move smoothly through these stages. During the *emergent literacy* (or *emergent reading*) stage, children with multiple disabilities do not have the same level of participation in their environment that would help them learn about letters and sounds as do typically developing children, nor do they have the experiential base of typically developing children or even children who are only visually impaired. This constrains them to the emergent literacy phase for an extended period of time. When students with multiple disabilities reach school and are introduced to letters and sounds, these letters and sounds lack the meaning that other typically developing children would associate with them, and thus the progress of these students in learning to read is slowed and often stops altogether. As a result, these students never move on to learning the skills in the *beginning reading* stage that they will need in order to develop the fluency in reading that will propel them into a more advanced reading level.

This book deals with the emergent literacy and beginning reading stages for children who have not been making typical progress through these stages. The

TABLE 2.1
Stages of Reading Development in Children

Stage of Reading Development	Definition
Emergent reading	Demonstration of the beginning stages of reading. Students at this level are beginning to understand that letters on a page produce specific sounds and that words are made up of letters.
Beginning reading	Development of a set of skills required for early elementary-level reading, including the ability to read connected text with a fluency rate of about 50–100 words per minute with comprehension. Students at this stage are transitioning from *learning to read* to *reading to learn*.
Advanced reading	Development of a set of skills required for reading at upper elementary levels. Students at this stage use reading for inquiry and knowledge building. They primarily use reading to learn new concepts.
Academic reading	An advanced reading level that is specific to academic content areas, including high school- and college-level reading. Students at this level have developed specialized vocabulary and concepts that are used in very specific academic content areas such as chemistry, physics, political science, and economics.

Source: Reprinted from Kamei-Hannan, C., & Ricci, L. A. (2015). *Reading connections: Strategies for teaching students with visual impairments* (p. 6). New York: AFB Press.

approach described is designed to move students out of the emergent literacy stage of their development and into the beginning reading stage. Depending on how well teachers are able to accomplish this, children may or may not progress into more advanced phases of their reading development.

To achieve this move into reading, I-M-ABLE differs from most traditional approaches to teaching reading. The previous chapter noted that the emphasis in beginning reading instruction with I-M-ABLE is on whole words, rather than letters. Unlike typical sight words, these whole words are extremely important and meaningful words for a particular student. However, learning to read words is only a part of what students need in the early literacy phase in order to emerge into literacy. The foundational skills that support the process of learning to read are phonological processing, print (or braille) awareness, and oral language (Whitehurst & Lonigan, 2003, p. 12).

Phonological processing—making use of the sound structure of oral language in order to learn how to decode written language (Wagner, Torgeson, & Rashotte, 1994, p. 73)—is developed through a child's hearing language and becoming sensitive to the sounds of language in conjunction with developing an awareness of how print or braille relates to these sounds. The three components of phonological processing are phonological sensitivity, phonological memory, and phonological naming. *Phonological sensitivity* is the ability to hear and manipulate the sounds of oral language; *phonological memory* permits a child to recall information about sounds; and *phonological naming* allows a child to retrieve information about sounds from permanent memory. *Phonemes* are the smallest units of sound in spoken language, and *phonemic awareness* is the ability to hear and manipulate these units of sound (Kamei-Hannan & Ricci, 2015, p. 10). Phonemic awareness skills are developed by activities such as rhyming games, letter-word-sound materials, and alphabet games related to words and sounds (Whitehurst & Lonigan, 2003, p. 24), which are played during early literacy instruction and which lead to the ability to pair sounds and symbols of the language (print or braille) (Hatton, Erickson, & Lee, 2010, p. 743; Whitehurst & Lonigan, 2003, p. 15). This ability to pair symbols and sounds translates into the ability to decode both familiar and unfamiliar words.

Oral language and concept development are learned in the early literacy phase through activities such as story time and shared reading (both at home and at school), with an emphasis on the meaning of the material being read, in environments that prominently display and provide access to the literacy medium, and through the development of experiences that promote knowledge and understanding of the sociocultural environment in which the child lives (such as vacations taken with the family; field trips to the fire station, the post office, the hospital, the farm; discussions about family life, etc.)

Older children may find that their literacy activities are directed more toward phonological processing and print (or braille) awareness, even though they may be lagging behind in oral language and concept development and still need to concentrate on the development of oral language and vocabulary from a wide variety of experiences. Teachers may find that they need to incorporate many of the activities of the early literacy phase with their students who are candidates for I-M-ABLE. Although this chapter focuses on assessing students and getting started, it also incorporates many activities that will promote students' growth into literacy.

First, however, the teacher needs to determine a given student's present level of functioning. And, in addition to assessing the student's capabilities, it is important to assess the student's learning environments to determine if they are optimal for the acquisition of the reading skills necessary for the student to succeed.

ASSESSING THE STUDENT

Before beginning any program with a student, it is important to know what he or she has already learned in terms of literacy acquisition. Which reading and writing tasks can the student perform? Collecting information that shows what a student already knows about reading and writing establishes a baseline of performance against which future progress can be measured.

A student may be able to read his or her name or one or two other words consistently but be unable to decode words, even simple words such as *hat* or *bat* without considerable assistance. A student may be able to recognize 20 braille alphabet letters inconsistently, while recognizing only eight or nine of those same 20 letters consistently. A student may or may not have been introduced to contractions and may or may not know some of the alphabetic wordsigns. Some students are able to write letters and certain words but are unable to read them. Other students have no writing skills. Some may have scattered skills in phonics or phonemic awareness. Some students may have had many stories read to them and have their favorites, but some may have had little exposure to written language and no exposure to braille. It is important to know what skills and exposure students have had so that these can be reinforced while new skills are being taught using I-M-ABLE.

Collecting Baseline Data

The Baseline Data Collection Form shown in Figure 2.1 provides the teacher with a simple way to determine just what the student is capable of doing related to reading and writing and how successful he or she is. The form collects information including motivation for learning braille; words that a student can read, including whether or not the child recognizes his own name; and letters the child can read. In addition, information is collected about what writing the child is able to do. (A copy of this form also appears in the appendix to this book.)

Motivation for learning to read and attitudes toward braille reading and writing are important, and collecting information about the student's motivation and engagement prior to starting a new approach is useful as a comparison once the

FIGURE 2.1

Baseline Data Collection Form

Student's Name: _____

Date: _____

I. Attitude toward Reading and Braille

Motivation Questionnaire

Directions: "I am going to ask you some questions about how you feel about things and I want you to answer with the words 'awesome,' 'just okay,' or 'yucky.'" (You may feel it is necessary to discuss what these words mean in order for the student to use them correctly.)

  Some things to keep in mind:
- Sometimes students like to perseverate on one or two of the answer words. Make sure they understand that they should be expressing what they really feel.
- Be aware that some students simply like the sounds of certain words and will say them just to hear the sound. For example, if the student is enamored with the word *awesome* used in the questionnaire, the teacher should substitute another, less appealing word for the student to use.
- A number of attempts answering some practice questions such as the following may be necessary.

Motivation Practice Questions

1. How do you feel about [a favorite food]? Is it awesome, just okay, or yucky?
2. How do you feel about [a food the student dislikes]? Is it awesome, just okay, or yucky?
3. How do you feel about [a best friend]?. Is he/she awesome, just okay, or yucky?
4. How do you feel about [an activity that the student really doesn't like]? Is it awesome, just okay, or yucky?

- Continue with the practice questions until you are sure the student is answering with what he or she really feels. Try to find some neutral things or activities so that the student can also answer with "just okay."
- It is important to keep the tone of your voice neutral so that you don't lead the student to answer a particular question in a particular way.
- Once you are sure the student understands how to answer the questions, record his or her answers on the sheet below after each question. (There are 12 questions.)

Motivation Assessment Questionnaire

Student's Name: _____

Date of Administration: _____

1. How do you feel when someone reads a story to you? You can say "awesome," you can say "just okay," or you can say "yucky."
    Circle one: Awesome   Just Okay   Yucky

2. How do you feel about learning to read braille?
   Circle one: Awesome   Just Okay   Yucky
3. How do you feel about learning to write braille?
   Circle one: Awesome   Just Okay   Yucky
4. How do you feel when it is time for braille reading or writing class?
   Circle one: Awesome   Just Okay   Yucky
5. How do you feel when your teacher asks you to read braille?
   Circle one: Awesome   Just Okay   Yucky
6. How do you feel when your teacher asks you to write braille?
   Circle one: Awesome   Just Okay   Yucky
7. How do you feel about the stories you read in reading class?
   Circle one: Awesome   Just Okay   Yucky
8. How do you feel about reading instead of playing?
   Circle one: Awesome   Just Okay   Yucky
9. How do you feel when your teacher asks you questions about what you have read?
   Circle one: Awesome   Just Okay   Yucky
10. How do you feel when you read a story?
    Circle one: Awesome   Just Okay   Yucky
    Have you ever done that?
    Yes   No
11. How do you feel when you read a story to a friend or a child who is younger than you are?
    Circle one: Awesome   Just Okay   Yucky
    Have you ever done that?
    Yes   No
12. How do you feel about taking a reading test?
    Circle one: Awesome   Just Okay   Yucky
    Have you ever done that?
    Yes   No

Teacher's anecdotal notes on motivation:

(continued on next page)

FIGURE 2.1 *(continued)*

II. Reading

Name Recognition: Three Names on a Line; Three Lines

- Use the child's name and two other names of similar length for this assessment. The additional names may be the names of friends or family members and should be similar in length to the student's name.
- Create a braille assessment sheet similar to the one in the example below. Use the child's name and two other different names in each of three rows, with three names per row and three spaces between each name. Mix up the order of the names from one line to the next.
- Give the following directions to the student: "Track across each line and find your name. You do not need to read the other names, just show me where your name is."
- As the student reads, refrain from providing any verbal or other assistance that might help the student identify his or her name, and do not indicate whether an answer is correct or incorrect. Spontaneous self-corrections may be counted as correct, but the last answer the student gives is the one scored (even if the first answer was right).
- Record the number of times out of three that the student is able to recognize his or her name.

Example

Assessment for *Jenny*. Distractors are *Brian* and *Mommy*.

Mommy	Brian	Jenny
Brian	Jenny	Mommy
Jenny	Mommy	Brian

Times student recognized his or her name: _____ /3

Word Recognition

Does the student consistently recognize any braille words? Please list them here:

Letter Recognition

Using the following sequence of letters, prepare a braille assessment sheet using three double-spaced lines of letters with three braille spaces between each letter.

```
g  k  v  t  b  e  o  l  h
z  i  j  p  f  a  x  c  r
u  s  q  m  w  n  d  y
```

- Give the following directions to the student: "Here is a sheet of letters all mixed up. There are no contractions. Please read the letters to me. If you do not know a letter, just say, 'I don't know it' and continue with the next letter."

- Refrain from providing any verbal or other assistance that might help the student identify the letters, and do not indicate whether an answer is correct or incorrect. Spontaneous self-corrections may be counted as correct, but the last letter the student says for a particular symbol is the one scored (even if the first answer was right).
- Record the student's answers as follows using the rows of letters shown above:
  - Write a + above each letter the student reads correctly.
  - Write the letter the student says above each letter he or she reads incorrectly.
  - Circle the letters the student does not know.
  - Do not count a letter as correctly recognized if the student misreads another letter as that letter. (For example, if the student says *x* for *x* and then says *x* for *y*, do not count either as correct.)
  - Record the total number of letters the student can recognize. _____/26

Contraction Recognition

Does the student recognize any contractions in isolation or in words? Please list them here:

III. Writing

Name Writing

Can the student write his or her name independently and consistently using the Perkins Brailler?

Yes   No

Word Writing

Can the student write any other words independently and consistently using the Perkins Brailler?

Yes   No

If Yes is circled, please list these words below and indicate whether the student uses contracted braille when writing these words by placing parentheses around the contractions used.

Letter Writing

Can the student write any letters of the alphabet independently and consistently using a braillewriter?

Yes   No

(continued on next page)

FIGURE 2.1 *(continued)*

> If Yes is circled, please write the letters below:
>
>
> **IV. Phonemic Awareness/Phonics**
> If there are no results in the student's record for a test such as the Dynamic Indicators of Basic Early Literacy Skills (DIBELS) or the Texas Primary Reading Inventory (TPRI), teachers should work with their school district to have one of these tests administered to the student.

approach has been implemented. The student's demonstrated motivation or engagement will help in determining whether the approach is working or if it might need to be altered in its implementation. When students are not successful in doing something, it is anticipated that they will not be as motivated to continue doing it (Malloy, Marinak, & Gambrell, 2010). Students whose teachers selected I-M-ABLE to use with them were often unmotivated to learn to read braille. In general, when students are learning something that is interesting and meaningful to them their motivation increases.

The simple 12-item motivation questionnaire included in the Baseline Data Collection Form (Figure 2.1) can be administered to students as a pre-assessment of their motivation for reading. There is also space for teachers to document their own opinions of student motivation or attitudes toward reading; they can also include anecdotal observed behaviors, which might indicate motivation. For example, "This student has been absent 85 percent of the days when we would normally have braille instruction" or "The student has told his teachers and his parents that he does not like braille." This questionnaire should be administered prior to implementation of the I-M-ABLE approach and included with the baseline data collected.

Phonological (including phonemic) awareness is considered a primary indicator of future success in reading (Lonigan et al., 2009; National Early Literacy Panel, 2008; National Reading Panel, 2000; Senechal, LeFevre, Smith-Chant, & Colton, 2001), therefore, collecting data on a student's phonemic awareness skills is an important first step if the data is not already available. An easy-to-administer assessment for phonemic awareness is the Texas Primary Reading Inventory

(TPRI; see the Resources section). However, there are other tests that school districts use which may assess phonemic awareness as well, such as Dynamic Indicators of Basic Early Literacy Skills (DIBELS; see the Resources section).

Collecting this type of data allows the teacher to establish a baseline that can be used to demonstrate progress once the program is underway. Teachers can benefit from creating an I-M-ABLE Student Record Book, perhaps using a three-ring binder, into which the Baseline Data Collection Form and other forms suggested throughout this book can be inserted, along with loose-leaf paper for keeping anecdotal comments on the student's interests and progress. For instance, teachers can make note of the games and activities that a student enjoys playing.

Although I-M-ABLE is designed for the older student who has mild to moderate cognitive impairments and has not been successful in learning to read braille, teachers may choose to use it as a means of motivating students who are adventitiously blinded and just learning to read braille and who may or may not have additional disabilities. Students who are younger or those who are more severely multiply impaired and who are still at the early literacy level may not be able to take advantage of all of the components of the approach without having more exposure to the typical activities that would occur during early literacy as mentioned above. With these students, the baseline data may contain more anecdotal information.

Collecting Information about the Student's Interests

After collecting baseline data using the form in Figure 2.1, the next step a teacher needs to take is to collect information about student interests.

One of the easiest ways to determine what students are and are not interested in is to observe them in their environments, both at home and in school. While it is often difficult to find time for observation, doing so pays off in huge returns when designing lessons for students. The more a teacher knows about a child, the easier it is to bring the student's experiences and interests into instruction. If it is not possible to observe the student at home, the next best thing is to have a conversation with the family about the student's interests and daily routine, special people who interact with the student, favorite family members, pets, activities the student particularly likes engaging in, and so forth. These conversations are important in the selection of key vocabulary words but also in establishing the child as an individual, with a specific set of experiences and preferences.

The teacher will want to learn a wide variety of information about the student, including the following:

- the student's friends within the school environment
- the student's school day routine
- the activities the student especially likes to participate in
- the things that excite the student as well as the things he or she especially dislikes
- any fears the student exhibits
- any appropriate or inappropriate behaviors the student may exhibit and when those behaviors are most likely to occur

While this practice guide does not include a form for collecting this type of data, it might be useful for teachers to include a page at the beginning of the student record book that has the heading "Important Anecdotal Information about [Student's name]." Teachers can even recreate the preceding list as a reminder of the type of information they are looking for about the student. They can then make note of that information, as well as information about the student's interests and progress, in the student record book. In that way, the teacher can maintain a record about the child's interests or experiences, which will help the teacher take advantage of teachable moments. Some guidelines for what to include in the student record book are included in Sidebar 2.1.

Assessing the Student's Learning Environment

In addition to assessing the student, in readiness for beginning I-M-ABLE, it is important to assess the learning environment in which the student finds himself or herself, as that environment can play an important role, either positive or negative, in helping the student develop literacy.

The learning environment for a child includes a number of factors:

- the intellectual climate of the environment (expectations teachers have for students in the classroom, incorporation of literacy activities into the classroom)
- the social/emotional environment (the student's role in the classroom, the number of individuals who work with the student, the interactions of those in the classroom with each other and with the student, the attitudes of other students and staff toward the student)
- the physical environment (type of classroom; setup of classroom; available space, equipment, literacy tools, and books; level of noise and other distractions)

The next section provides information on what to look for in each type of environment, along with the types of activities that would ideally be present for the

SIDEBAR 2.1

Guidelines for the Student Record Book

The following list contains elements for which teachers should keep records and track student progress. Some of the records may come from tests, and others may simply be anecdotal records that teachers record in the loose-leaf pages of the Student Record Book.

1. All assessment results, including those from the Baseline Data Collection Form (Figure 2.1).
2. Anecdotal information on a variety of topics: the student's interests, words the student wants to learn to read, experiences that the teacher knows the student has had and wants to read about, etc.
3. A record of words introduced, words mastered, and when they were mastered.
4. A list of contractions the student has learned or is working on.
5. A record of phonemic awareness/phonics activities the student has completed or is working on.
6. Writing: the tools used by the student, when the tools were introduced, and the student's knowledge of the conventions of writing.
7. The ways in which the student uses reading and writing for functional purposes.
8. A collection of the stories the student has written and a portfolio of stories that the student likes to read.
9. A list of the books the student has read.
10. An ongoing record of the student's reading rate (words per minute).
11. Anecdotal information about the student's enjoyment of reading (monitor closely).
12. A record of the student's success in using prosody in reading.

I-M-ABLE student. The teacher can make a note of which activities are missing and come up with a plan for how to incorporate missing activities into each environment.

Intellectual Climate

When students struggle with learning to read, teachers' expectations of the level of literacy they will achieve often diminish. Unfortunately, this can create a vicious cycle. The less achievement expected of students, the fewer literacy activities or the less instruction provided. Work-related or daily living skills activities often begin to fill up more and more of the student's curricular time, without any attempt to incorporate related literacy activities.

Rather than de-emphasizing literacy, what is often needed is a change in the approach that is being used to instruct students. I-M-ABLE, because of its ability to engage students at their own levels, helps enhance the expectations of both teachers and students. Teachers need to have high expectations for their students and expect them to improve. If they do not expect a student to develop literacy skills, teachers will be less motivated to provide, and engage that student in, experiences leading to literacy.

In some instances, attempts to promote literacy in a classroom can in fact be lost on students. If the stories being read to them are beyond their experiences and comprehension capabilities, and if they are read to without any attempt to engage them in learning the new vocabulary and concepts that would be necessary to understand the story, students may simply tune out and disengage during story reading time or they may sometimes even act out.

Students who are blind and have additional disabilities have many gaps in their conceptual understanding. Stories can be used to expand their conceptual learning and their knowledge base, providing teachers first determine the knowledge and experiential base children bring to the story, and then make sure the story is meaningful to them. Students also love having fairy tales read to them. It is important for teachers to ensure that students understand the concept of fantasy and fairy tales, to overcome any lack of conceptual experience.

The following questions can help assess whether the stories being read to a student will promote his or her learning:

- Does the student have a background of experience with the concepts in the story? For instance, if reading *The Hungry Caterpillar*, a favorite children's book, determine if the child has ever had experience with caterpillars. If not, try to use the book as a way to include that experience. Caterpillar kits, commonly available at science stores, can permit students to have an actual experience with caterpillars—to hold them in their hands, feel the cocoons they make, and experience their hatching into moths or butterflies.
- How heavily does the book rely on pictures to make the story interesting? Can a set of objects be substituted for the pictures? Some of the books available from the American Printing House for the Blind (APH) have tactile drawings that make the books interesting for students with visual impairments.
- Is the book available as a print/braille book (picture book that has braille overlays on the pages)? The more braille a student has exposure to the better. If not, can a braille copy of the book be made available to the student to read along with as the story is being read?

- What interests the student? The more closely a book is related to a student's interests, the more likely the student is to enjoy hearing the book read.
- Is the book a "predictable book"? Predictable books have sentences or phrases that repeat. Children love to be able to repeat portions of the book when someone is reading to them. Sidebar 2.2 gives some suggestions of the types of predictable books that children love to have read to them.

The Resources section at the end of this book includes websites that provide lists of predictable books that teachers can select from according to their student's interests, as well as a listing of publishers of children's books in braille (and some in print/braille).

In addition to commercially available children's stories, stories created by teachers in both print and braille based on the experiences of their students can help students understand that reading can have meaning for them. These stories can be constructed from typical daily routines, field trips that a class has taken, stories that family members have shared with the teacher, or they can be created

SIDEBAR 2.2

Types of Predictable Books

- **Chain or circular story.** Plot is interlinked so that the ending leads back to the beginning. Laura Numeroff's *If You Give a Mouse a Cookie* is a good example of a circular story.
- **Cumulative story.** Each time a new event occurs, all previous events in the story are repeated. The well-known tale of the Gingerbread Man is a good example of a story that is cumulative.
- **Pattern story.** Scenes are repeated throughout the story with some variation, as in the fairy tale *The Three Billy Goats Gruff*.
- **Question and answer.** The same or similar questions are repeated throughout the story. *Brown Bear, Brown Bear, What Do You See?* by Bill Martin is a good example of this type of text.
- **Repetition of phrase.** Word order in a phrase or sentence is repeated. Margaret Wise Brown's classic *Goodnight Moon* is an example.
- **Rhyme.** Rhyming words, refrains, or patterns are used throughout the story, such as *Is Your Mama a Llama?* by Deborah Guarino.
- **Songbooks.** Familiar songs with predictable elements, such as a repetitive phrase. The classic song *Over in the Meadow* has many predictable elements.

Source: Reprinted by permission of Pearson Education from Vacca, J. L., Vacca, R. T., Gove, M. K., Burkey, L. C., Lenhart, L. A., & McKeon, C. A. (2012). *Reading and learning to read* (8th ed., pp. 275–276). Boston: Pearson.

around holiday events that are familiar to students. Stories can have multiple pages with one or two sentences per page in both braille and print. Students can help create tactile drawings or paste objects on the pages of the books to enhance the story, as in the following example:

> Leah loved jewelry. Her teacher created a story book for her to read that included all of her favorite types of jewelry. The book had the title *Leah Loves Jewelry* on the cover. There was a page for each type of jewelry that Leah loved. Each page had a simple sentence on it like "Leah loves ankle bracelets" or "Leah loves her necklace." Also on each page was a pocket that had to be opened to find the piece of jewelry. Each page had a different type of pocket with a different opening. For example, on the page for the sentence "Leah loves ankle bracelets," the teacher glued a small zippered pouch into which she placed an ankle bracelet. Leah and her teacher would read the sentence at the top of the page, and then Leah could zip open the pocket to find the ankle bracelet. Then she would put it on her ankle. On the page that had the sentence about the necklace, the teacher created an envelope for the necklace that sealed shut with Velcro tabs. Leah and her teacher would read the sentence and then Leah could pull open the tabs to find the necklace and put it on. And so it went with all of the various pieces of jewelry. At the end of the story, Leah and her teacher could either work their way backward to the beginning or start at the beginning again and this time Leah would take off each piece of jewelry that the sentence on the page mentioned and put it back in the pocket. This was one of Leah's favorite story books.

Through reading and rereading these meaningful stories students can learn how to manipulate books, what braille feels like on a page, and what written language sounds like. Teachers can talk with students when reading about how to hold the book, how to turn the pages, how to locate the braille on the page, how to track the lines of braille, and any other concepts they feel the student needs to learn about reading that are related to the story or the book.

In addition to providing meaningful stories for students to enjoy, another aspect of a student's intellectual climate relates to whether the student's literacy medium is available to him or her. While the availability of specific media might be considered part of the physical environment, it is actually part of the intellectual environment, in that learning is promoted when a student has access to his or her literacy medium. Many students who are blind do not have the same exposure to braille in their environment as sighted students do to print. No matter what approach is used to teach braille reading, the creation of opportunities to see braille

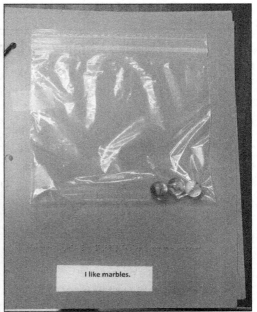
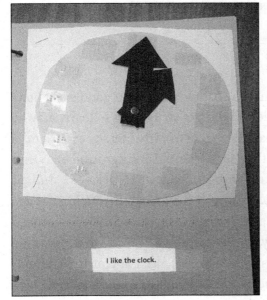
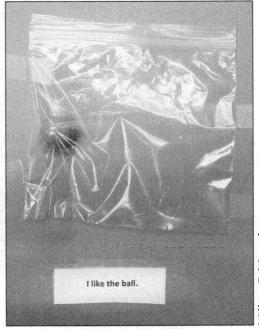

Photos from the pages of a meaningful book created for a student by his teacher.

in use in the environment is critical. Sidebar 2.3 and Figure 2.2 provide suggestions for teachers to follow to assure that the student's environment provides rich opportunities to experience braille. Remember that just having braille in the environment isn't enough. The child must be shown where the braille is and what it means. The teacher's mantra should always be "fingers on braille!"

> **SIDEBAR 2.3**
>
> ## Creating a Braille-Rich and Language-Rich Environment
>
> 1. Provide for exposure to words and letters in braille.
>   a. Create labels in the environment in braille. Invite students to explore where braille is in the environment.
>   b. Read stories from books in braille and print.
>   c. Create meaningful story books for students based on their own experiences and read them to the students.
> 2. Model uses of braille reading and writing using a variety of different types of tools, such as:
>   a. braillewriter
>   b. electronic braillewriter
>   c. slate and stylus
>   d. electronic notetaker
>   e. refreshable braille display
> 3. Provide language and words for students to explain what is happening in their environment.

All of the suggested activities found in this chapter are simply good early literacy experiences. In fact, the types of students who are struggling to learn may be struggling in part because they have not had the extent of early literacy experiences that other children may have had. Or, their experiential background may not have permitted them to participate in a meaningful way. A 16-year-old student may not, for a variety of reasons, be functioning at his or her chronological age when it comes to reading and writing. Teachers need to facilitate what is required in order to help students develop literacy, while keeping in mind what might be developmentally appropriate for the mental and experiential age of the student, and at the same time keeping in mind the chronological age of the student.

Social/Emotional Environment

When beginning any new approach with a particular student, it is important to assess the social/emotional environment of the classroom in which the student is currently placed. How will the classroom teacher and others who work with the student view this new approach? Will they see it as an imposition on their routine? Will they view it as potentially good for the student? How do they view the student himself or herself? Do they see the child's potential? Do they feel that literacy is important for the student or that it will be a waste of time? What are the

FIGURE 2.2

Checklist for a Braille-Rich Environment

- Braille is visible on open charts and bulletin boards around the room.
- Braille is incorporated in each area of the classroom.
- Braille is presented in a standard size and displayed in a way that makes location and reading easy for students.
- Braille represents words that are familiar to children because of daily activities, thematic inquiries, and special experiences.
- Student's names are brailled (and printed) on their cubbies, placemats, and other items.
- Name cards and other brailled words are available for students to copy or read.
- Students are encouraged to write their own names or letters from their names on their artwork.
- Mailboxes are available for each child and family, encouraging communication between home and school and showing children that written messages are an integral part of classroom life.
- A newsletter in braille and print describing a student's activities is shared with the children and sent home regularly.

Source: Adapted from Strickland, D., & Schickendanz, J. (2009). *Learning about print in preschool: Working with letters, words, and beginning links with phonemic awareness* (2nd ed.). Newark, DE: International Reading Association.

other students in the class like in relation to the student you will be working with? Are they more advanced intellectually? Less advanced? Are they general education students? Is the class a special class such as a cross-categorical disability grouping? Do the students all represent a particular disability? Are they verbal or nonverbal? How do they interact with the student, and how does the student view the other students in his or her class?

In addition, it is important to know how the student's parents fit into this mix. How do they and the students' teachers relate to each other? Is there a good working relationship? Do the parents wish to have the child learn braille? Are they supportive of the use of a new approach?

These questions about the social/emotional environment are important to ask and to note prior to actually working with a student. The teacher should take some time to assess the social/emotional climate and identify which factors contribute to buy-in by all who work with the student. Documenting the assessment will also provide some baseline data to use when later determining whether there were any changes in the social/emotional environment after the I-M-ABLE approach was implemented.

Ultimately, if parents and others who work with the student are open to using a different approach and if they see the student as having potential, more progress can be expected, as more people will want to work with the student on his or her own special curriculum. The following examples show the difference a supportive social/emotional climate can make:

> Hannah's teacher of students with visual impairments was also her classroom teacher. She felt lucky in that Hannah's mom was supportive of the use of I-M-ABLE with Hannah. The mother followed Hannah's progress carefully, began learning braille, and was able to provide new words for Hannah at home, which she then shared with Hannah's teacher. In addition, when Hannah began demonstrating some success in learning to read, word of her new abilities quickly spread throughout the school. Hannah's teacher often had visitors come into her classroom to see Hannah in action. Hannah got lots of supportive comments during these visits, which reinforced her good feeling about learning braille.
>
> •••
>
> Another student, Jeannie, whose teacher of students with visual impairments was not her classroom teacher, did not get any follow-up with I-M-ABLE activities in the classroom. The classroom teacher felt that the literacy instruction that she provided for her class was enough for Jeannie, and that Jeannie simply wasn't ready to learn to read. The stories the teacher was reading to the children were very advanced and quite over their heads, so they often disengaged during reading time and simply sat quietly. The teacher misinterpreted this passive behavior as interest.
>
> Jeannie's mother was ecstatic at her daughter's progress in learning to read whole words and in her daughter's new interest in learning to read braille after Jeannie's teacher of students with visual impairments began I-M-ABLE instruction. As the year progressed, the classroom teacher still wasn't willing to do any follow-up with what Jeannie's mother knew was proving to be successful for her daughter. Jeannie's parents decided to change Jeannie's placement to a different school where the classroom teacher had indicated support for the approach and where follow-up would occur. Although Jeannie's teacher of students with visual impairments was concerned about not being able to continue her I-M-ABLE instruction with Jeannie, she was able to help the new teacher understand the I-M-ABLE approach, and Jeannie's progress in learning to read braille continued in her new placement.

Once a student begins making progress, it is important to assess how teachers, staff, and parents view that progress. Do they celebrate this success? Do they feel threatened by seeing the progress a student is now making, perhaps because they feel guilty that progress had not been made sooner? All members of the team must be assured that they are valuable, and efforts must be made to help them take ownership of the new progress. Buy-in from everyone who works with the student is important, as the more praise and support the student receives from everyone, the more success is likely to continue to occur.

The Physical Environment

The physical environment in which the student will be taught is just as important as the intellectual and social/emotional climates. So many times, teachers who work one-on-one with students—as is required by this approach—do not have space to adequately teach the students or store the materials that are required. Teachers of students with visual impairments are accustomed to working in closets, or to being moved around from room to room. Often the size of the room is less important than whether it is free of distractions. Students simply have more trouble concentrating when they have to put up with the band practicing on one side of them, or hearing another student screaming in the room next door through the wall. Teachers should assess the environment in which the new approach is to be implemented and make reasonable requests for space to store equipment, furniture that fits the child, and enough peace and quiet to permit learning to occur.

FREQUENCY OF INSTRUCTION

Determining how often instruction will take place is another issue to consider. How much time per week will the teacher be able to teach the student using this new approach? In recruiting teachers for an initial study of I-M-ABLE (Wormsley & McCarthy, 2013), it was requested that they commit to two days per week for at least half an hour a day with their student, and that they could then work with others to have them reinforce I-M-ABLE in the classroom. Almost as soon as students began showing progress, teachers realized that they needed to spend more time with them in order to facilitate the highest level of success possible for each student.

Two of the teachers had over half an hour to an hour each day with their students, in an environment that was typically free of intrusive distractions. These students, although both very different from each other, made steady progress throughout the course of the year (Wormsley & McCarthy, 2013). Another teacher whose student made good progress was able to convince the child's classroom teacher and paraprofessionals to follow some set games and lessons that she left for the student when she was not there. If children who have no other disabilities receive anywhere from two to three hours of literacy instruction per day, it makes sense that children who find it more difficult to learn to read should have more literacy instruction, not less. The Delphi Study results reported by Koenig and Holbrook (2000) recommended anywhere from one to two hours per day on a daily basis for beginning braille readers. However, that isn't what is typically found in school settings when teaching braille to children who have additional disabilities.

INVOLVING OTHERS

Part of getting started with the I-M-ABLE approach is to determine who else is willing to become involved in helping use this approach with a student. Having a meeting early on with the other staff involved with the student to ensure their buy-in to the approach is important. At that time it will be necessary to educate them as to the rationale of the approach and solicit their involvement in observing the student to determine likes and dislikes, or to ask what they already know in this area. At this meeting, discuss where you will work with the student, when you can have time for the others involved with the student to observe you, how you are working with the student so that they can help replicate the various aspects of instruction, and determine where in the classroom the materials that the student will be using will be kept for his or her easy access.

As the student learns some simple tasks, such as using the Talking Card Reader or sorting cards into baskets (described in later chapters), these activities can be incorporated into practice time in the classroom. The easiest way to ensure this incorporation is to have the activities written out in large type with explicit instructions and directions for how to proceed to help those who are working with the student be consistent. Place these instructions in a location where they are easily retrieved, such as on the desk where the Talking Card Reader is being used, or on the wall above the student's desk. Prior to assigning someone to work with the student, that individual would benefit greatly from observing a lesson with the student to see how things are done.

Communication with the classroom staff and parents is important. Communication doesn't always have to be verbal, but it does have to be consistent. One teacher cut off the top right-hand corner of the stories that the student was able to read independently. The paraeducator who worked with the student could then immediately recognize whether the story she was to help the student with was one that she could expect the student to read without assistance, or whether the student might need her help.

GETTING STARTED

A tool for teachers to use when they are beginning to implement any of the components of I-M-ABLE, including the early literacy activities mentioned in this chapter, is the Fidelity of Implementation Checklist found in Figure 2.3 and the Appendix. This checklist provides a listing of what an observer would see the teacher doing for each of the components if the teacher is following the approach according to its principles of implementation. Referring to this checklist regularly is also a way in which teachers can assure themselves that they are following the approach faithfully. Teachers can copy this checklist for themselves and use it to critique their own teaching of each of the components of the approach.

Teachers of students with visual impairments know they need to help students become more independent, and that they need to let students do things for themselves. However, when teachers are beginning this approach, because there are so many new things to consider, they may find themselves forgetting to provide opportunities for students. Teachers may want to videotape themselves while teaching in order to ensure they are providing opportunities for independence. The video will also be a good way to document what students are doing. Teachers can use the Fidelity of Implementation Checklist (Figure 2.3, also in the appendix to this book) to evaluate whether they are implementing the approach correctly.

This chapter included the types of assessments that will help teachers evaluate an older student who has not yet been successful in reading, or a younger student who has characteristics that might suggest that he or she will have difficulty in learning language as well as learning to read (ESL students for example). The examples of activities for early literacy will need to be incorporated into the student's I-M-ABLE program in order to help the student continue to make progress in literacy. The following chapters will discuss the various components of I-M-ABLE and will provide teachers with a road map to follow for implementing each of these components.

FIGURE 2.3

I-M-ABLE Fidelity of Implementation Checklist

1. Getting started and incorporating early literacy instruction
   - ☐ Exposes students to words and letters in braille
   - ☐ Models uses of braille reading and writing
   - ☐ Provides language for students to explain what is happening in the environment
   - ☐ Reads meaningful stories to students
   - ☐ Promotes concept development
   - ☐ Introduces and allows students to explore writing tools
   - ☐ Sets up a learning environment that is conducive to student learning
   - ☐ Involves others in teaching students

2. Selecting key words
   - ☐ Selects key vocabulary words with student input
   - Generates key words from:
     - ☐ Conversations with students
     - ☐ Observation of students
     - ☐ Consultation with other key people in students' lives (parents, other teachers, paraprofessionals, etc.); verifies with students
   - ☐ Responds to student selection of additional key words and incorporates student preferences in lessons
   - ☐ Uses filler words derived from need (e.g., story-making requires them)

3. Introducing key words
   - ☐ Ensures first several words are tactually distinct in length, features, etc.
   - ☐ Provides multiple copies of word cards for each word
   - ☐ Creates word cards correctly (lead-in lines as long as possible, proper spacing, correct braille contractions)
   - ☐ Tells students what words are; avoids testing
   - ☐ Demonstrates to students how to use the word cards (find lead-in line, use both hands together, track across the line—a space after the lead-in line indicates that a word will follow)
   - ☐ Introduces entire words; points out features of words
   - ☐ Provides ample repetition
   - ☐ Uses nonslip surface under cards
   - ☐ Assures proper furniture fit

4. Instruction in tracking
   - ☐ Incorporates key vocabulary words already introduced into initial instruction
   - ☐ Incorporates meaningful "story"
   - ☐ Ensures lines are at least double-spaced and of equal length
   - ☐ Ensures lead-in lines mirror those used in word cards; spaces before and after key vocabulary words

- ☐ Demonstrates to students how to move their hands on the lines (both hands together like on the word cards)
- ☐ Demonstrates to students how to move from one line to the next (initially both hands go back over to the beginning of the line they are on and then down)
- ☐ Asks students to indicate in some fashion when they have found a word or words
- ☐ Uses nonslip surface under braille paper
- ☐ Ensures number of words per line matches student progress (initially no more than one per line, gradually increasing as competence in word recognition increases)
- ☐ Ties progression to more difficult tracking to students' capabilities (includes lines of varying lengths, tracking of sentences in stories of multiple lines, single spacing when appropriate)

5. Reinforcing word recognition through games
- ☐ Reviews words to be used in games (words should be mastered by student)
- ☐ Teaches students how to play the game (include a practice game)
- ☐ Ensures others who might play games with students know how to play
- ☐ Keeps records on which games students and others know how to play, and what words they are able to use when playing the game, as well as who students play the game with

6. Writing instruction
- ☐ Uses backward chaining to assist students in learning to use the brailler
- ☐ Incorporates writing into each section of the approach
- ☐ Teaches correct finger position on keys (no curling under or lifting up of fingers)
- ☐ Teaches students to look at what they have written after writing

7. Letter/contraction instruction
- ☐ Uses initial letters from key vocabulary words to isolate for letter recognition
- ☐ Creates letter cards for introducing the letters
- ☐ Plays games with letters in isolation
- ☐ Plays games with letters and words together
- ☐ Uses contractions from key vocabulary words to isolate for contraction recognition
- ☐ Explains what the contraction looks like and what letters it stands for; uses the letters to identify the contraction (for example, "this is the 't-h-e sign,' not the 'the' sign")
- ☐ Introduces other words with the same letters or contractions for students to read

8. Phonics instruction
- ☐ Is responsive to students (student interest in a particular letter/sound combination should generate acknowledgement on the part of the teacher); builds interests into subsequent lessons
- ☐ Utilizes key vocabulary words in building phonics lessons
- ☐ Takes advantage of onset/rime patterns in key vocabulary words

(continued on next page)

FIGURE 2.3 *(continued)*

☐ Takes advantage of grapheme/phoneme patterns in key words
☐ Makes new words from old; Word Wall activities (uses APH Word Playhouse when appropriate)
☐ Plays games with phonics; "tell me the real word" (Chunk Stacker games)

9. Creating stories with students
☐ Uses key vocabulary words to create (with the students) meaningful stories for him or her to read
☐ Uses filler words to create stories as they are needed
☐ Reads stories together with students until students can read the story independently
☐ Creates a folder for the stories students have generated and can read
☐ Provides opportunities for students to practice reading stories to others

10. Creating functional uses for braille
☐ Takes advantage of routines
☐ Takes advantage of holidays
☐ Creates uses related to the child's capabilities

11. Expanding students' reading/writing vocabulary
☐ Adds to reading/writing vocabulary from discussions
☐ Uses stories to create new words to read and write
☐ Uses phonics activities to create new words to read and write

12. Building fluency
☐ Incorporates daily practice in automaticity of word recognition
☐ Models prosody in reading stories
☐ Provides support for building fluency by using echo reading, tape recordings, and other appropriate supports such as repeated readings
☐ Focuses on correct phrasing for stories as appropriate
☐ Provides opportunities for students to read continuous text on a daily basis

13. Maintaining records
☐ Records daily lessons on Lesson Summary Sheet form (see Chapter 4 and Appendix)
☐ Maintains records of student mastery of words, and progress under each category above
☐ Helps students understand progress and feel successful
☐ Translates progress into performance on IEP goals

CHAPTER 3

Helping Students Select Key Vocabulary Words or Phrases

Key vocabulary words are emotionally laden words that engage a learner. Sylvia Ashton-Warner, who created the key vocabulary approach for Maori students who were having difficulty learning to read, wrote:

> No time is too long spent talking to a child to find out his key words, the key that unlocks himself, for in them is the secret of reading, the realization that words can have intense meaning. Words having no emotional significance to him, no instinctive meaning, could be an imposition, doing him more harm than not teaching him at all. They may teach him that words mean nothing and that reading is undesirable. (Ashton-Warner, 1963, p. 44)

COLLECTING AND IDENTIFYING KEY VOCABULARY WORDS

The following are some suggestions for ways that a teacher can collect words that a student will use in learning to read.

Engage in Discussions with the Student

Whenever possible, engage students in discussions about what they like to do and what things they are interested in at the moment. "Interview" students about what their day is like, what they most like doing, who they most like interacting with, and also what they are afraid of. Ashton-Warner found that words related to children's fears and sex were the most important words for them. Her children selected words such as *knife, fight, skeleton, kiss,* and *love,* among others. These words "burst them into reading" after little or no success with sight words from the New Zealand primers that she had been using with them. When children can select the words they want to read, and when these words are emotionally powerful for them, they are more engaged and motivated to read.

Observe the Student

Observe students to see what they react to in their environment and note the words that relate to these experiences. Some children may not be able to express to their teacher what interests them due to their lack of language capability. However, observing children who are jiggling with delight or exhibiting other nonverbal signs that something excites them could help identify a possible key vocabulary word that should be added to the list. Even reacting in a way that shows fear or dislike can create something to talk about, and the word for whatever is eliciting such a reaction may be a very powerful word. Sidebar 3.1 provides some examples of words that were identified as key vocabulary words, as well as one that seemed to be one, but wasn't.

Talk to Others in the Student's Life

Solicit the help of parents and other teachers, teacher assistants, family members, and others who interact with the student to help suggest words that would be of high interest to the student. Soliciting the help of others to identify key vocabulary words serves several purposes. It helps the teacher learn more about the student and what he or she is interested in, and it engages parents and others in the process of using the I-M-ABLE approach with the child, permitting them to demonstrate what they know about him or her. It helps build the idea that using the I-M-ABLE approach is a team effort, and that they have the capability of participating and providing the teacher with important information.

Learn the Student's Favorite People and Activities

Discuss school, home, and community activities in which the child enjoys participating, as well as people with whom he or she enjoys interacting. The daily routines both at home and in school are important to discuss. Knowing the child's favorite people and activities can often suggest names or words that the student may want to learn. In addition, it provides the teacher with some information about the types of experiences the child has had and enjoyed which might form the basis of stories that the teacher and child might write together later on in the process of using this approach.

Use the Form for Collecting Key Vocabulary Words (see Figure 3.1 and the Appendix), or a similar method, to collect vocabulary words that are within the student's realm of experiences.

SIDEBAR 3.1

Identifying True Key Vocabulary Words

Marcos, a young boy who was totally blind with developmental delays, had very little expressive English language due to his learning English as a second language. His teacher of students with visual impairments, Ms. D., discovered that he loved riding the bus. Together they sang songs about riding the bus, and they created a taped story about riding the bus. Marcos enjoyed and participated in these activities and they gave him much-needed language. Ms. D. determined that *bus* might be a key vocabulary word for Marcos, and introduced it to him using a set of flash cards. However, Marcos simply wasn't interested in learning to read the word and showed this by disengaging. He put the word card in the "finished" basket.

In another attempt to involve Marcos in reading, Ms. D. observed that when she said "beep beep" as the sound that the bus's horn makes, Marcos began jiggling up and down on his tiptoes and flapping his hands with excitement. She created a set of flash cards with the word phrase *beep beep* on them. Upon introducing the word *beep beep* to Marcos, Ms. D. was delighted to find that he was engaged in learning to read and talk about this word for an extended period of time. She knew from Marcos's behavior that this time she had found a key vocabulary word that would engage him and draw him into reading.

Another teacher observed her student playing with a vibrating ball with bumps on it. As she watched his joy over playing with this ball, she also noticed that he was repeating the words *bumpy ball* over and over again, while laughing and giggling. She had already introduced several key words to the student to which he had reacted well, but when she introduced the word phrase *bumpy ball* to him, he could hardly sit still. Afterwards she reported to others, "Now I know how to tell for sure when I have a key vocabulary word!"

BUILDING AND ANALYZING THE KEY VOCABULARY LIST

Following the process just described should net lots of words that are meaningful to the student. As new potential key vocabulary words emerge, the teacher can add them to the list. The secret to success in using this approach is to be able to tell which words elicit true engagement and emotional response from the child. These words should be starred or highlighted and are the key vocabulary words that will be the most motivating for the student to learn to read. These are also most likely the words that students would select for themselves.

Through interviews with family members, other teachers, and the student, the teacher will collect a comprehensive list of words. Most of these words will be important to the student, and all can be used at some point in instruction.

FIGURE 3.1

Form for Collecting Key Vocabulary Words

Questions for Gathering Vocabulary	Home Setting	School Setting	Community Setting
Who are the significant people the student interacts with?			
Which words describe the student's daily routine?			
What are the student's hobbies, favorite things, and activities?			
Which words describe the student's work activities and chores?			

Source: Adapted with permission from Wormsley, D. P. (2000). *Braille literacy curriculum.* Philadelphia: Towers Press.

However, as the examples in Sidebar 3.1 showed, finding first words that are extremely motivating and meaningful will help the student to engage and increase his or her motivation. The impact of the selected words can be gauged by reading them to the student. Judge the words by the reaction from the student. Once it has been determined that the vocabulary words collected are true key vocabulary words or phrases, instruction can then be designed around them. Although the list of key vocabulary words may be small at the start, the more time spent working with the student and getting to know him or her better, the more words that will add to the list.

All that is needed to get started is one key vocabulary word! Pick the word that appears to be the most significant word for the student. Get affirmation from the student that he or she wants to learn to read that word. Since the idea of this approach is to build in success from the very beginning, the words used in the beginning should have very different distinguishing tactile features from one another. Once the first word has been selected, then the next word should be different in certain gross tactile features such as length, braille features, initial letters, and any other distinguishing features that can help the student tell them apart, at least initially. To help determine what word to teach second, choose a key vocabulary word that is tactilely distinct from the first word used, braille the second word, and then compare it to the first to see how different they feel from one another. Determine what distinguishes one from the other and help a student identify that difference. With the first few words, this gross difference is critical in achieving successful recognition.

Each time a new word is added, consider how to help the student identify tactile differences. Continue the process with as many words that are tactilely distinct from each other as possible. Words that have too many tactile similarities will be harder for the student to distinguish from one another and may lead to frustration. Keeping the words tactilely distinct at the very beginning of learning to read assists the student in learning how braille words feel, promotes the successful recognition of one word from another, and helps the student develop tactile sensitivity.

Marcos, the student in Sidebar 3.1 who learned *beep beep*, also wanted to learn *alligator*. The two words, while both long words, were tactilely distinct when written in braille: *beep beep*, ⠃⠑⠑⠏ ⠃⠑⠑⠏, has a space in the middle of the two words; *alligator*, ⠁⠇⠇⠊⠛⠁⠞⠕⠗, has one dot and two "lines" after it at the beginning of the word. These distinct features helped Marcos learn to distinguish these words from each other. Another word, his name, was short and also easily distinguishable from the other two words. With these three words, he was on his way to being able to add more and more.

Sidebar 3.2 contains an example of a collection of words and phrases that are potential key vocabulary words or phrases for another student. An analysis of these words and phrases following the guidelines just suggested resulted in several words that were deemed to be the most meaningful and the most tactilely distinct from each other. Those words or phrases are highlighted in bold in Sidebar 3.2.

INCLUDING CONTRACTIONS

When collecting vocabulary words it is inevitable that some of the words will contain braille contractions (as seen in Sidebar 3.2). Some of these contractions will help make the words tactilely distinct from other words in the list. Some teachers feel that contracted braille is too difficult for students with additional disabilities to learn to read. Because of the manner in which the key vocabulary words are introduced, however, contractions are simply part of the word and are not taught explicitly until after the student is capable of recognizing and discriminating among quite a few words. Learning to read these words occurs much more easily than teachers initially anticipate.

SIDEBAR 3.2

Analyzing Potential Key Vocabulary Words

The following words and phrases were selected as potential key vocabulary words for a student. Those that were deemed to be the most meaningful as well as the most tactilely distinct from each other are highlighted in bold.

Word	
Elsa	⠨⠑⠇⠎⠁
Frozen	⠨⠋⠗⠕⠵⠑⠝
Anna	⠨⠁⠝⠝⠁
Kristoff	⠨⠅⠗⠊⠎⠞⠕⠋⠋
Mom	⠨⠍⠕⠍
Dad	⠨⠙⠁⠙
Elf [pet poodle]	⠨⠑⠇⠋
Frosty [drink from Wendy's]	⠨⠋⠗⠕⠎⠞⠽
Uggs	⠨⠥⠛⠛⠎
chocolate chip cookies	⠡⠕⠉⠕⠇⠁⠞⠑ ⠡⠊⠏ ⠉⠕⠕⠅⠊⠑⠎

I-M-ABLE introduces words to students using the contractions that occur naturally within the word; therefore, contractions are taught as students comment on them, or as they occur. There is no hierarchy of contraction introduction; when the contraction is in the word, the contraction is used. When it comes time to spell the words, teachers should refer to the contractions by their letters. For example, in the word *motion* the teacher would not call the contraction "dots 5-6 *n*" but rather refer to it as the "t-i-o-n sign." When talking about writing it, the teacher would also refer to it as the "t-i-o-n sign" and continue to explain that we make this sign with dots 5-6 and then *n* (dots 1-3-4-5) on the Perkins Brailler.

The list of key vocabulary words that have been collected will continue to be added to throughout the course of the year as teacher and student have more and more conversations about what is meaningful to the student. Initially, students may not be able to say what words they want to learn, but once they catch on that their interests influence the lessons and that they can direct their own learning, they will begin to ask for words to learn. When students do begin to ask for words, teachers should be sure to incorporate them into lessons as soon as possible. Ignoring a request for a word is like discounting the student's involvement in his or her own learning.

Teachers will want to be prepared to have some fun and exhilarating conversations and to learn more about their students than they ever dreamed they would know! Each student will have different word and phrase lists and different experiences. The teacher will want to have a notebook handy (for example, the student record book described in Chapter 2) to keep track of notes from conversations with the student and to have a convenient place to record new potential key vocabulary words. These conversations provide the teacher with information about the background knowledge that the student is bringing to the reading experience as well as information that the teacher may later use to write stories, introduce games, and so forth.

Once the teacher has a list of key vocabulary words for the student, and has determined which words are meaningful enough and tactilely distinct enough to begin with, the teacher is ready to begin the work of teaching the student to read. The next chapter discusses the steps for introducing these words to the student.

CHAPTER 4

Introducing Key Vocabulary Words and Phrases

The selection of the key vocabulary words or phrases is an important step in beginning to use I-M-ABLE. While collecting these words the teacher will have begun to learn a great deal about what is interesting to the student and what words might stimulate him or her to want to learn to read braille. The previous chapter showed how to analyze the list of words and pick several that are tactilely distinct from each other. Once the teacher has collected this set of words, it is time to select the first word to introduce. It is important that the student feels that he or she has a part in the choice of that word. The teacher can ask the student to select which word he or she wants to learn first, or based on the interests of the student, can provide the student with a reason why a particular word is a good one to learn first.

Once the first word has been selected, the word that is most easily distinguished from it should be the next word introduced. Sidebar 3.2 highlighted a list of potential key vocabulary words. From these words, three stood out as being tactilely distinct from one another: *Frozen, chocolate chip cookies,* and *Uggs*. The student chose to learn *chocolate chip cookies* first. *Chocolate chip cookies* is more than one word, is very long, and has spaces between the three words. *Uggs* is the shorter of the two remaining words, and provides a good second word to introduce. The two words are shown here in SimBraille and in print with the contractions underlined.

(<u>ch</u>ocolate   <u>ch</u>ip   cookies)

(U<u>gg</u>s)

Looking at or touching the braille makes it obvious how different these braille words are from each other.

When introducing these first key words or phrases to a student it is important to discuss how they feel different from each other. The teacher may need to help the student express this difference in words. The student will learn that words may be different in length (long or short), dot density (lots of dots or open spaces) or both. The words may also be different because of some significant tactile feature that is unique to one word but not another—for example, the straight up and down line of the letter *l*. The adjectives used to describe these tactile features will depend on the student's vocabulary, but it is not necessary to pre-teach these concepts—they can be learned at the same time as the key vocabulary words are being learned. Learning to use descriptive words for how the brailled key vocabulary words feel will help the student learn what these descriptive words mean (if the words are not already familiar ones).

CREATING THE KEY VOCABULARY WORD OR PHRASE CARDS

I-M-ABLE uses brailled flash cards for introducing new words to students. These cards can be taken home, used in playing games, kept in a box so students can see how many words or phrases they are learning, or shared with friends.

Creating word or phrase cards is simple. Braille flash cards are created with lead-in lines of dots 2-5 before the word and similar lead-out lines after the word. The lead-in line is designed to assist students with tracking to locate the word on the card. Once the student finds the lead-in line on the left-hand side of the card, he or she begins moving his or her fingers across the line to the right to locate the word. It is important to insert a space after the lead-in line and before the word, and also after the word and before the lead-out line, so that the student can learn to identify where the word begins and where it ends by the spaces around it. This also helps to introduce or reinforce the concept of a word as having a space on either side of it. The top right-hand corner of each card is cut off to make sure the cards can be positioned correctly. Since braille can look different upside down, and yet still feel like braille, it is important to ensure that the cards are all right side up. Sidebar 4.1 contains instructions on how to create word or phrase cards.

Students who are not efficient braille readers often scrub the braille characters, moving their fingers up and down on each character in an attempt to recognize it. Because I-M-ABLE is concerned more with the feel of the whole word, teachers should encourage students to move smoothly across the lead-in line to the word and to keep moving across the word and beyond to the lead-out line. This focus on the whole word helps develop smoother tracking movements. Beginning with

SIDEBAR 4.1

Creating Word or Phrase Cards

The following instructions explain how to create word or phrase cards. The lead-in and lead-out lines and the spaces before and after the words are very important. Without the spaces, students may have difficulty finding the beginning and end of the word.

Card Size

- Use at least 3 × 5-inch cards—4 × 6-inch cards are even better; the longer the better.
- Long, narrow cards allow word cards to be kept together with sentence cards in the future.

Positioning

- Cards should be oriented horizontally.
- Cut off the top right-hand corner of the card to assist the student in positioning the card—be consistent.
- Use a line of dots 2-5 to lead into the word.
- **Include a SPACE before the word.**
- Write the word.
- **Include a SPACE after the word.**
- Use a line of dots 2-5 to lead out to the end of the card.

Create Numerous Cards for the Same Word

The cards don't have to be identical; nor do they need to be extremely different in terms of where the word is placed. Using numerous cards for the same word

- prevents learning a word from some unique feature on a card like a bump or rough spot
- allows for multiple viewings of the word, similar to the multiple times a sighted child can look at a flash card
- introduces a degree of variety into the lesson, as the student is not constantly looking at the same flash card and has a set of them to manipulate

Incorporating Writing

If students already know how to write braille, let them help make word cards using either a Perkins Brailler or a slate and stylus.

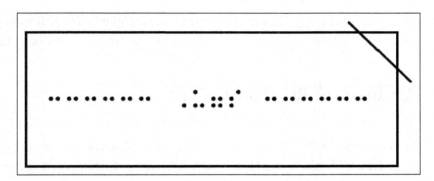

A flash card showing the braille word *Uggs* with lead-in and lead-out lines and a space before and after the word.

whole-word recognition rather than letter recognition reduces the student's tendency to scrub.

INTRODUCING THE FIRST KEY WORD

Once the initial words have been selected, and a number of word cards created for each, it is time to introduce the first key vocabulary word to the student. This is not a time for playing guessing games. The teacher should tell the student what the word is on a card every time they read it, even if the word doesn't change from one card to the next. In introducing the words to the students, teachers have two skills they want to perfect:

1. Tracking the word smoothly and correctly without scrubbing.
2. Learning how to talk about how the word feels in braille: identifying the significant features of the word so that the student will be able to recognize the word from those features when he or she sees it again, and so the student has the vocabulary to compare it to other words he or she is going to learn.

Initially teachers will need to devote some time to teaching students how to track across the words smoothly, while still recognizing the spaces before and after the word. How long this takes will depend on the students. Teachers need to carefully monitor where the child's fingers are to be sure they are covering the tops and bottoms of the braille cells in the words. In combination with teaching smooth and accurate tracking, teachers will want to talk with students about how the words feel. Teachers may have to help students develop vocabulary for this description. I-M-ABLE refers to this as "teaching the language of touch."

As students gradually develop smooth tracking skills with their fingers covering the braille cell fully, the instruction in tracking and finger position can be faded out, and more time can be spent on describing the critical features that allow students to recognize the words and differentiate them one from another.

TEACHING HOW TO TRACK CORRECTLY

When learning how to track a word, students should be taught to use both hands and as many fingers as possible (preferably all four) on the line while reading a card. This will take some time when students are first learning how to look at the words on the cards, but once students get the idea of how to move their hands and fingers, they can then concentrate a bit more on the words themselves. There are several key points to remember about teaching efficient use of the hands when reading key vocabulary word or phrase cards.

Nonslip Surface

First, make certain that there is some sort of nonslip material under the cards that will prevent the cards from moving around on the table or desk. Without a sticky surface under the cards, students might end up having to use one hand to anchor the word card, while using the other to read, or else the teacher might have to hold the card still. Neither of these is a good option. If the student holds the card, then one hand will miss out on learning to read; if the teacher has to hold the card, he or she won't be able to take notes on the student's success in reading or concentrate on how the student is moving the hands and fingers.

Some teachers have found material large enough to cover the student's entire desk, which not only keeps the word cards in place but also keeps other items from slipping off the desk, such as baskets that are used for sorting the word cards or other materials being used in the lesson. The type of tacky-feeling rubberized shelf liner that is sold in dollar stores is often equally as effective as more expensive materials such as Dycem. Check the material before buying to be sure it feels fairly tacky, as some types of shelf liner are smoother and, therefore, less effective in keeping the cards in place.

Proper Finger Position

Proper finger positioning involves using both hands with as many fingers as possible on the braille line and utilizing the pads of the fingers rather than the tips to feel the braille cells. Encourage students to keep all four fingers of both hands in contact with the braille line as much as possible. Although promoting this pattern of finger usage may take some time initially, it is worth developing to ensure correct positioning. If the student cannot keep all four fingers on the line, the teacher will want to make sure that at least the two index fingers and possibly the middle fingers are in contact with the line. Having both hands involved in reading will eventually enable students to learn to separate their hands when reading, thus making the hand movement pattern more efficient.

When first introducing words to students and teaching proper hand and finger usage, the teacher will want to make sure the first joints of the student's fingers are flattened so that the finger pads are able to feel the full width and length of the braille cells underneath. Using all four fingers of each hand involves curving the fingers to allow for them to line up, and sometimes this curving results in students' using the tips of their fingers instead of flattening the first joints of the fingers so that the pads are fully on the braille. It is important to ensure that students use the pads of their fingers because when students use the tips of their fingers, they may not feel the full braille cell and will miss out on key features of the letters and the word. The teacher may need to model what is expected and give the students time to become comfortable with the way they need to position their fingers.

Make sure the students' fingers cover the tops and bottoms of the braille cells they are reading. Even after the teacher is confident that a student is using good finger position, frequent spot-checks are recommended. Sometimes students will use their index fingers to read and raise the other fingers in the air rather than keeping them in contact with the lines of braille. They may be tense and concentrating on what they are feeling with their index fingers. The teacher should encourage students to relax and reinforce all four fingers at least on the page if the students are not able to have them on the braille line itself.

Smooth Tracking

As previously noted, teachers need to make multiple flash cards for each word, and the lead-in and lead-out lines with spaces before and after each word give students the path to follow to the word and past it to the end of the line. Encourage students to keep their hands and fingers moving smoothly across the line from left to right, over the lead-in line, the space, the word or phrase, the space, and the lead-out line. The spaces are critical in helping the student distinguish the word from the lead-in and lead-out lines. If students pause on a feature, remind them that they can always go back to the beginning of the line and look at the word again as many times as they wish if they are trying to remember or find a particular feature.

If students consistently have problems keeping their fingers centered on the lead-in line, try showing them where they should feel the line in the center of the pads of their index fingers. If they still have difficulty, use a line of dots 1-3-4-6—⠹ ⠹ ⠹ ⠹ ⠹ ⠹ ⠹ or a row of the letter *X*—for the lines. Encourage the students to keep their finger pads in the middle of the "tracks" so they can feel both the tops and bottoms at the same time. Using the *X*'s puts the fingers in the correct position to feel the tops and bottoms of the cells in the word when they reach it. Whichever lead-in or lead-out line is decided on should be used with all of a student's words. Otherwise, if one type of lead-in or lead-out line is used with one word and a different one with another, the student may come to associate each line with a particular word that has nothing to do with the word itself. This also detracts from the student using the braille word itself for word recognition.

For some students who have been unsuccessful at learning to read braille, scrubbing may have become a habit. If students have already learned some letters when this approach is started, they may be accustomed to scrubbing up and down on the letters to identify them, and they may apply this scrubbing technique to the new words they are learning. Under these circumstances, the teacher can remind them that the goal is to get the feel of the whole word, not individual letters, and to be able to recognize that word by distinct features. These features are best identified when the students keep their fingers moving across the word smoothly and do not move them up and down on the individual braille characters. If students begin scrubbing, the teacher can have them go back to the beginning of the line and start over, concentrating on keeping their tracking smooth.

Focus on the Whole Word

Initially the teacher should not expect students to recognize letters or contractions in the word and should not ask students to identify the letters they feel. Teachers who have taught using a traditional approach may find it difficult to keep from asking students about the letters or contractions that are under their fingers, but keep in mind that I-M-ABLE is being used because a student has not responded well to the traditional approach. Even if the students are capable of identifying letters, asking them to isolate characters and letters at this point will only slow down their ability to recognize the entire word as a whole. Teachers can explain to the children that they can read the word as many times as they need or want but that they should keep their fingers moving smoothly over the word rather than scrubbing up and down. Generally, when the lead-in lines are used, the students do not attempt to scrub. Most teachers report that when students begin using key vocabulary word cards and realize that they are not being asked to identify individual letters or characters but are being encouraged to keep moving smoothly across the word, their tracking improves and any scrubbing which might have been present disappears.

During each lesson, teachers should keep track of whether the student is scrubbing and any other difficulties the student has maintaining contact with the line. If a student is using hands and fingers correctly and demonstrating smooth tracking, that should also be noted.

TEACHING THE LANGUAGE OF TOUCH

Students may or may not have the language to describe how a braille word feels. When being introduced to a new word or phrase card, a student should be asked to move across it and look at it several times. The teacher needs to determine if the student can feel the distinguishing features of the word as his or her fingers move over it. Then the teacher and student need to decide together on some language that describes these features.

Depending on the feature, teachers could ask students if they feel there are lots of dots in the word or phrase, or if there are openings. Are the dots all clumped together or are they spread apart? Is the first thing felt at the beginning of the word a tall shape? Where does it fall on the finger pad? At the top? In the middle? If a student doesn't initially recognize a key feature of the word (for example, that the first letter is tall), the teacher should mention the feature and model the language that could be used. Sometimes showing students what the letter or contraction looks like using a Swing Cell (a model of a braille cell with removable pegs, available from the American Printing House for the Blind and discussed in more detail in Chapter 8) or some other means of showing an enlarged cell enables students to see what they can expect to feel when they are reading. Using descriptive words for the letter or contraction will model for the student how to talk about it.

At this point students do not need to know what letters are in the word. If a student happens to have learned some letters and recognizes them, the teacher can praise him or her for remembering and then repeat the feature that helped the student recognize the letter. However, if a student doesn't already know any letters, he or she simply needs to be able to recognize and describe what is felt at the beginning of the word or phrase and then what other tactilely distinct features exist in the word.

Tying these tactilely distinct features to the word or phrase is important. For example, for the word *pizza*, ⠏⠊⠵⠵⠁, the teacher might say that it starts out with a straight or tall shape with an extra dot at the top. Try to determine if the *zz* (⠵⠵) pattern with its two open spaces right next to each other is easy for the student to recognize. Look for other features that stand out in the words being examined with the student. Before beginning to teach any words, pick out one or two significant features of the words or phrases that the student can use to recognize the word and come up with some terms that might be used to refer to them.

It is also important to make sure that at least one of the features for each word occurs at or near the beginning of the word. (Later on the teacher will expand on the number of significant features in the word to include shapes of the characters themselves, but initially it is enough to give the students some language for what they are feeling.) Efficient braille readers read the first two or three characters of a word and then use these letters along with context and their experience to help them figure out the word. This speeds up the process of reading braille (Kusajima, 1974; Millar, 1997). So while it might be possible for a student to notice something at the end of a word as a significant tactile feature, it should not be the only significant feature a child is taught to recognize in that particular word. Teachers should try to focus the students on what they feel at the beginning of words along with the feel of whole words. The tactilely distinct feature at the end then becomes a redundant clue rather than the only clue to the word.

The teacher will want to listen carefully if students attempt to describe feeling something distinctive. Students may not have accurate words to describe what they feel so the teacher may have to work with them to agree on language that will then become meaningful to them. Doing so expands the student's own vocabulary. The teacher can make a note of the language constructed with the student so that that vocabulary can be used for as long as it is appropriate.

Through this approach, rather than teaching tactile discrimination using pre-reading materials such as various textures and shapes that don't resemble braille, the student is learning tactile discrimination and perception of braille using the braille itself. This means that the instruction is immediately relevant to the task at hand.

Initially it may be difficult for the teacher to focus on both descriptive language and proper hand placement and tracking. If this is the case, the teacher can try alternating between the two. It is important to ensure that students are feeling the tops and bottoms of the braille cells. Otherwise, when discussing what they should be feeling, they may not be able to relate it to what is under their fingers because they aren't feeling the whole character. When developing the language of touch, it is not possible to ignore hand and finger position on the braille.

In summary, the following are some tips for teaching the language of touch:

- Give students a chance to explore the cards as many times as they wish. Encourage exploration.
- Reinforce the fingers moving across the lines.

- Provide multiple cards for each word. This allows the students to practice organizing the stack of cards and learn how to get a "fresh" one when ready.
- Agree upon language for distinguishing features.
- Remind students frequently what the present word is and how it feels using the agreed-upon language.
- Talk about what the word means to the students as they read the word.
- Ask the students to say the word out loud when they move their hands over it.

INTRODUCING THE SECOND KEY VOCABULARY WORD

Once the student has explored one word in this manner, has been able to read and say the word multiple times, and can describe how he or she knows what the word is (by discussing its distinguishing features), it is time to introduce the second word. This word, which the teacher selected carefully to be tactilely distinct from the first one, will allow the teacher to tell whether the child has actually learned to recognize the first word. Without having two words to differentiate it is not possible to determine if the child can recognize either of them.

The same process is used with this second word, with the teacher introducing it as he or she did with the first. The teacher will create the word cards, talk about how the word feels, help the student develop the language for the distinct features, make sure the student is keeping fingers in the correct position, and allow the student to read the word as many times as desired. When the student has completed this exercise with two words, the teacher can start to compare them.

To begin the comparison of the first two words, the teacher has the student place one card for each word on the nonslip surface in front of him or her. The teacher reminds the student what the two words are, then talks with the student about the features of the word on the left first, and then of the word on the right. (If the student isn't sure of left and right, the teacher doesn't have to stop and teach those concepts in isolation, but rather can introduce or reinforce the concepts of left and right within the context of comparing the two cards that the student has learned.) Here is an example of what the teacher side of this dialogue for comparing two word cards might look like:

> You have learned *pizza*, ⠏⠊⠵⠵⠁, and *Nathanial*, ⠠⠝⠁⠞⠓⠁⠝⠊⠁⠇.
> You have the word *pizza* on the left, so let's take a look at *pizza*.
> Remember we talked about how *pizza* feels at the beginning of the
> word? (Wait briefly for student to respond, but if he or she doesn't, then
> supply the language again. Reinforce this with the student.) Now let's

look at *Nathanial*. Remember we talked about how it feels? Tell me about that. (Pause for what the student might remember and then affirm if the student supplies the language, and if not, supply the language for the differences again.)

Okay, now let's see if we can talk about how *pizza* and *Nathanial* are different. Take a look at *pizza* again. There is that tall letter at the beginning and some open space in the middle and one dot at the end. Then let's look again at *Nathanial*. It has that single dot at the bottom, which is a capital dot because Nathanial is a name. Whose name is this? (Let the student respond.) And what else makes it different? (If the student doesn't indicate it is longer than pizza, remind the student.)

Nathanial doesn't begin the same as *pizza*, but it ends with a tall letter, right? And it is longer.

The teacher should continue on in this vein until he or she senses that the child is catching on to the descriptive language for the distinct differences and can recognize the words when presented with them separately without the teacher saying which words they are. The following section presents the next step in the process, assessing whether the student can differentiate the two words independently.

NEXT STEPS
Tracking Multiple Lines of Braille

After the student has practiced reading the two words with the teacher telling him or her initially what the words are, it may be helpful to give the student a chance to read some short tracking stories focused on each of the two words. Tracking stories focus on a word the student is studying by creating a "story" to prompt the student to seek a known key vocabulary word on a page of braille containing multiple lead-in and lead-out lines with the key vocabulary word on each line. Creating stories such as this to teach tracking will also reinforce the recognition of words that students are already familiar with in a different and fun way (see Chapter 5 for more information on developing and using tracking stories).

Beginning Word Recognition

The next step is to assess whether the student can differentiate the two words independently. One way to do this is for the teacher to say to the student, for example, "I have the words *pizza* and *Nathanial*. Let's take a look at them again." Put the two word cards next to each other on the table in front of the student on a nonslip mat, and examine them again, moving from one to the other and back again. Talk about what makes the words different from each other and then take the two word cards and put one on top of the other. Ask the student to pick up the two word cards and place them back on the nonslip mat, one on the left and one on the right. Ask the student to take a look at them, and wait to see if he or she is able to identify each word. If the student doesn't identify the words after a few seconds of looking at them both, ask the student to look at the one on the left again and then tell him or her what the word is. Again, reinforce what the significant features of the word are with the student. The teacher might say, "That word is *pizza*. Remember it has the tall letter at the beginning and is a short word?"

Once it is obvious that the student is able to differentiate the words, remove the two word cards, take the multiple copies of the two words, and mix them up. Place the pile of the mixed-up words in front of the student and explain that the pile contains the two words *pizza* and *Nathanial* mixed together. Show the student where the pile of words is and have the student select the first card and place it on the mat. It is important to let the student take control of the desktop and the pile of words. Avoid placing every card one at a time in front of the student. The more the student does independently, the more he or she is directing his or her own learning. Let students have every opportunity to be in control.

Wait for the student to position the word card, and then wait for the student to identify the word. If the student doesn't identify the word after two to three seconds, tell the student what the word is, making it seem as if this is part of the lesson, and reminding the student of the word's distinguishing features. Try to avoid asking the student directly what the word is, instead say something like, "Okay now you have the word card in front of you and it is the word . . ." and then pause to see if the student will provide the word. The assumption is that if the student knows the word, he or she will tell the teacher. If the student doesn't tell the teacher right away, the teacher can say the word as if simply finishing his or her sentence. The teacher can then reiterate the distinguishing features of the word. Each time the student selects another card from the pile, the teacher can wait a bit longer to see if the student can identify the word.

Testing for Word Recognition

When the teacher is confident that the student can recognize the two words and differentiate them from each other, it is time to test for word recognition. Prior to doing so the teacher may ask the student if he or she thinks a review of the words would be a good idea before taking a test on them, as just described. (The teacher can decide whether to call it a test, or a probe, or something else, depending upon how the student reacts to the words.) For the test, the teacher presents the student with the stack of cards mixed up and asks the student to read the word cards. The teacher should keep track of the number of attempts, the number of correctly read words, and make a note of anything that may need reinforcing with either word. Ideally, the teacher's assessment would take place at the end of a lesson where the student was learning or comparing these words. However, if there isn't time at the end of a lesson, the next time the teacher works with the student, the teacher should be sure to first compare the words side by side before starting the assessment.

The teacher should be sure to praise the student for his or her terrific work. Remember that feeling successful promotes engagement and motivation to continue to learn.

Mastery

When testing students on their word recognition, strive for 100 percent accuracy on each word before adding on additional words. A student may perform an assessment with 100 percent accuracy, but this may not necessarily mean that the student has "mastered" the words included in the assessment. Mastery means that the student can recognize the word 100 percent of the time when it is encountered, not just on an assessment but also when reading.

Once the teacher feels that the student can accurately recognize the first two key vocabulary words, the teacher can move on to another word. From now on the teacher will be introducing one new word at a time, and then comparing and contrasting the new words with the previously learned words to learn more and more significant tactile features.

Achieving 100 percent accuracy will assist the student when encountering these words in stories, and will assist in developing fluent reading. However, the teacher will find that as the number of words the student has learned grows ever larger, a comprehensive assessment of all of the words that the student has learned will need to be performed in order to determine if mastery has been maintained.

The teacher should begin taking mastery probes on a monthly basis of all of the words that have been introduced to the student in order to determine how many words the student can recognize automatically. The example of the completed Form for Recording Words Learned, Practice Dates, and Mastery in Figure 4.1 shows the date that each word was introduced as well as the accuracy scores on the monthly probes. The accuracy scores reflect whether the student read the word correctly (identified as a plus sign) or incorrectly (identified as a minus). Ben's teacher began working with him in November, and the form shows his progress on both key and filler words up through January. Filler words are words that are needed when students are beginning to read simple stories using their key vocabulary words. These words are called filler words because they fill in the spaces between the key vocabulary words to create sentences. For example, the words *I* and *like* are filler words that allow a sentence such as "I like candy" to be written using the key vocabulary word *candy*. (Filler words are discussed in more detail in Chapter 7.)

Determining the Pace of the Lessons

Until the teacher begins introducing words and performing assessments for mastery, he or she will not know how many words can be introduced in a week, or even in a lesson. If a teacher is in doubt about the pace of a lesson, he or she should ask the student. A simple question like, "Do you want to learn to read *chocolate* today?" may give the teacher all the information needed. Keeping lessons flexible and varied in content so that the student is not doing the same thing every day are important factors for the teacher to consider.

Fingers Numbing Out

Be alert for when students' fingers might begin to "numb out." It takes a while for students who are not accustomed to reading a lot of braille to build up the tolerance for the sensation. Initially it may only take 20 minutes or less for students' fingers to become numb, depending on how much time they actually have their fingers on the braille. Once this numbing occurs during a lesson, the teacher will notice a decline in the student's ability to perceive what he or she is feeling. The teacher may even be able to anticipate the numbness occurring because the student will begin to get more and more tentative about identifying a word. A student who might have been able to identify the distinctive features in a word may suddenly no longer be able to recognize a word he or she has identified many times before.

FIGURE 4.1

Form for Recording Words Learned, Practice Dates, and Mastery Filled Out for Ben

Student's Name: Ben

Word[a]	Intro Date	Practice Dates[b]	Mastery Date	Sep Accuracy[c]	Oct Accuracy	Nov 21 Accuracy	Dec 21 Accuracy	Jan 21 Accuracy	Feb Accuracy	Mar Accuracy
bumpy ball K	11/1		11/21			+	+	+		
the F	11/14		12/17			−	+	+		
scratchy K	11/22		12/9				+	+		
ball K	11/28		12/13				+	+		
red F	11/28		12/7				+	+		
blue F	11/28		12/7				+	+		
yellow F	11/28		12/7				n/a	+		
likes F	12/2		1/23				n/a	−		
see F	12/2						+	+		
(contract.) like K	12/7		12/13							
Mommy K	12/13		12/15				+	+		
cupcake K	12/14		12/21				+	+		
we F	12/16		1/5				n/a	+		
and F	12/20		1/5				−	+		
snow K	1/5		1/13					+		
it F	1/10		1/26				−	n/a		

[a] K = Key; F = Filler
[b] When a word has been introduced it is practiced every school day after that; sometimes two times a day if I am not at his school. His classroom teacher or assistant sits with him as he reads his cards and/or stories.
[c] + = Recognized; − = Missed

Introducing Key Vocabulary Words and Phrases 57

It is important for the teacher to alert students to what this experience feels like and let them know when their fingers might be numbing out. Otherwise students may feel that braille is simply too difficult for them. When numbing occurs, or when it is even suspected, stop asking the student to recognize the words and try some different activities for a while before going back to working with word and phrase cards.

Teachable Moments

Take advantage of "teachable moments" to move students ahead toward the end goals of recognizing letters and contractions. The following is the type of dialogue that might occur when a teacher is paying attention to teachable moments (also known as being responsive to students):

Teacher: Okay, here is your word, *lollipop*. I have a stack of word cards for you to look at and they all have the word *lollipop* on them.
(Student takes first card.)
Teacher: Good, you found the corner cut and you have your card in the right position for reading. Your hands are nicely placed also. Let's move your hands across the card and find the word *lollipop* and then keep on moving across the card until you get to the end.
That was nice. Now let's do it again and see if you can tell me anything you notice about this word. What is the word?
Student: Lollipop.
Teacher: Right—one of your favorite snacks!
Student: (Moves hands across word but doesn't say anything.)
Teacher: Good, now try it again and see if you notice anything.
Student: (Moves hands across word—again nothing.)
Teacher: When you move your hands across the card this time, see if you can find the straight up and down line at the beginning of the word. Can you find something like that?
Student: Yes, here. (Keeps finger on first *l*.)
Teacher: Great! Let's try reading it again, and this time when you say the word *lollipop* think about that straight up and down line at the beginning. It reminds me of the stick on your lollipop.
Student: (Laughs; moves hands across the word.)
Student: I feel the stick. What flavor is this lollipop?
Teacher: I don't know. What is your favorite flavor?

STUDENT: Chocolate. I love chocolate lollipops.

TEACHER: Maybe we can learn the word *chocolate* some time! (Writes on the lesson plan the suggestion for the word *chocolate* as another word to learn.)

STUDENT: (excitedly) Yes, yes! That would be good!

TEACHER: There are actually two other sticks in the word *lollipop* when you move across it. Can you find them? They are right next to each other!

STUDENT: I see them. And more after!

TEACHER: Yes, there are two other straight up and down letters, but they are a little different from sticks because they have an extra dot at the top. Here, let's look at the Swing Cell and I'll show you the difference. (Shows student the *l* and then makes the *p* for the student to see the difference.)

TEACHER: When you get more used to reading braille you will be able to feel the difference between those very easily. So take some time and read the word *lollipop*. Look for the sticks and see how many straight up and down sticks there are in this word. There are lots of straight up and down lines in it, aren't there?

STUDENT: Yes there are.

TEACHER: Can you tell me what sound *lollipop* starts with?

STUDENT: (Makes sound for /l/.)

TEACHER: That's right. And the letter we use for that sound is an *l*. You are reading lollipop which begins with *l*. That is the straight up and down stick that you are seeing. An *l*.

STUDENT: Hmmm.

TEACHER: We'll talk more about that later. You are doing a nice job reading the word lollipop.

REVIEW LESSONS

It is important to once again review the words to which the student has been introduced before they are used for any games or activities. Reviewing the words does not mean testing. In a review lesson, the teacher indicates to the student that they are going to be looking again at the words that the student has learned to read. The teacher introduces each word by placing the word card in front of the student, asking the student to look at the word, waiting a bit to see if the student volunteers what it is, and then either verifying that the student is correct, or telling the student what the word is. If the student volunteers an incorrect word, simply tell the student that it was a good try and tell them what the word is. Say something like, "That was a good try. This word is "[insert word]" and the way you remember it is that you feel "[insert significant feature]."

At the beginning, the teacher should review no more than three words at a time. As the student begins to recognize more and more words, the teacher can increase the number of words reviewed. Each time a word is reviewed, the teacher should compare it with the others that have been reviewed. By the end of the review lesson, the student should have the words firmly fixed in his or her mind as to the features of each and should be able to discriminate them from each other with minimal help from the teacher.

LESSONS AND GAMES FOR REINFORCING WORD RECOGNITION

When the student can accurately recognize two or more key vocabulary words, he or she should be able to play some games with them. The games will reinforce word recognition as well as provide fun for the student. The teacher might want to start with a discussion, asking the student if he or she knows how to play any games. A couple of new key vocabulary words may come out of this discussion. The teacher can let the student know that he or she can learn to play some games with the word cards he or she has learned, and that these games can be played at home or with another student, teacher, or teacher aide. The teacher may ask the other individuals who work with the student to observe the teaching of the game, so that they understand how to play and know which words they should use when playing with the student. (If the aides or others don't know braille, write the print words somewhere on the cards in an unobtrusive place where students with low vision cannot see them, along with the key tactile features and where they are located).

Tips for Playing Games

Here are some helpful tips for playing games with students:

- Think about having students change position and move during games and activities. Not all activities have to be done sitting down. Try to modify the games and activities so that they can involve standing up or moving around. For example, a student can sort while standing up at a counter or play Concentration (described in the next section) while standing up. This gives the student some activities that involve his or her whole body.
- Encourage peers to join in. Peers can assist students when they are practicing reading their word and phrase cards if the words or phrases are labeled

in print on the cards on the back. They can also play matching games or Concentration with the student. This makes the reading game enjoyable while at the same time reinforcing the act of reading the words or phrases.
- Play games and activities *after* students have mastered key words. Remember that it isn't as much fun for a student to play a game when he or she is constantly misreading the words. These games should be played with words that the student consistently reads correctly.

The games described in the following section are suggestions. Teachers can modify and switch them up with the student to provide variety and avoid boredom.

Concentration

The game Concentration can be played with two or more players and anywhere from 4 to 12 word cards placed braille-side down in a grid layout. A large sheet of shelf liner with Wikki Stix—flexible wax-covered pieces of yarn that stick in place—separating the cards from each other will help the student place and replace the cards. (Or the teacher may find a commercially made frame that works for the size of the word cards he or she has created.) Each player needs a container for holding matched card pairs. The first player turns over one card and reads it, then turns over and reads another card. If the two cards match, the student takes the two cards and places them in his or her container. If they don't match, the player makes sure any braille readers playing are able to feel the board to see where the cards turned over are located. The student then turns the cards back over so each is again braille-side down. Players must try to remember where each word card is on the grid. The next player then takes a turn. The winner is the player with the most cards in his or her container when all the cards are matched.

Sorting Games

Given a pile of word cards, the student sorts them into one of two containers, depending on the word. Initially, the containers might simply be one container for each word. The student has to read the card out loud and place it in the right container. As the student learns more and more words, more containers can be added, or the original two containers might represent word categories instead of specific words—for example, all the word cards that are names of friends go in one container and the other word cards go in another container. The categories will depend on the words the student has selected to learn to read.

Which Two Are the Same?

This game involves sets of three word or phrase cards, two that are the same and one that is different. The teacher creates several of these sets and paperclips each set of three cards together. The student has a basket with the sets of cards to the left and an empty basket on the right. The student takes one set of cards from the basket on the left, takes off the paperclip, spreads the cards in front of him or her on a nonslip surface, and reads the cards. The student puts the card that is different in the basket on the right; the remaining two cards that are the same are clipped together with the paperclip and put in that same basket on the right. The teacher can see if the student matched the two that were the same correctly by checking the sets with the paperclips on them. When the original basket is empty, the student can ask to have someone check to see how many points he or she received. This can also generate a conversation about how many sets there were. If there were ten correctly matched sets, then ten points would mean the student was a winner!

Mad Libs

To play Mad Libs, the teacher can create some simple stories and omit a word or two in each sentence, or select stories from a Mad Libs booklet with the blanks already provided (these are often sold in toy stores). The teacher gives the student the two (or more) words that are known in a mixed-up pile of word or phrase cards. The teacher tells the student that he or she is going to start reading a story and when there is a pause, the student should read the first card in the pile. Since the words will most likely make no sense in the context of the story, this is guaranteed to bring some laughs!

Pick the Word That Makes Sense

The teacher gives the student two or more known words and has the student place them in front of him or her. Prior to beginning the game, the teacher should braille some sentences with blanks where one of the words might make sense but the other will not. The teacher reads the sentences to the student, saying "blank" where the blank occurs, then asks the student to select the word that would make sense to use in the blank. (The teacher might have to model this if students aren't used to using the word blank in this way.)

As students learn more words, the teacher can use a larger stack of word cards and can ask the student to draw word cards and read them until he or she finds one that makes sense in the sentence.

Share Word Cards

When a teacher has two students using the I-M-ABLE approach, the teacher can have the students share their word cards with each other. Each student picks a card or two from the other student's words, and the two students make a sentence or two with combinations of those words. They can write the sentence on a brailler or tell someone their sentence so that that person can write it down.

Monster Munch

This game is more suitable for younger students. The teacher gives the student a pile of word or phrase cards that the student knows. After the student reads a word or phrase card, he or she feeds the word or phrase card to the Monster (a box with a slit in it for a mouth that faces the student, and that is open on the teacher's side). If the student is correct, the Monster (teacher) makes a noise like "yummy." If the word is not correct, the Monster makes spitting noises and spits the card back out. (This may take some manipulating.) A word of caution: sometimes students like the spitting noises more than the "yummy" noises, so they make errors just to hear the word "spit" out! (As an art project, students may enjoy creating their monster and decorating it. However, this activity should be done during art, not during literacy time.)

Fishpond

This game requires the talking GlowDice and Score Card, available from the American Printing House for the Blind (see the Resources section at the back of the book). The teacher spreads the word cards on the table and has the student press the GlowDice to determine how many cards he or she needs to read for a point. Keep track of points using the Score Card. Another way to do this is to have lots of cards in the pile, and have the child just read from the top until he or she has read as many words correctly as are needed to for the point.

Talking Card Reader Activity

The teacher can use a talking card reader as a way for students to practice reading and checking their key vocabulary words and filler words. The talking card reader is a type of tape recorder that uses cards with magnetic strips on them to record words or sentences. The word or phrase can be brailled on the card and the card run through a slot in the device to record the word or phrase. The card can then

Introducing Key Vocabulary Words and Phrases 63

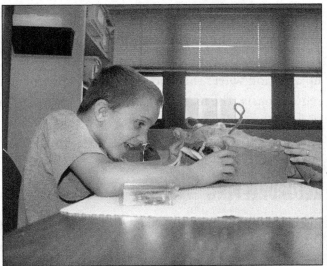

Student playing Monster Munch: reading the word card (top); and feeding the Monster the word card (bottom).

be reinserted through the slot on the card reader to play back the recorded word or phrase. (To extend the life of the cards—which can be expensive—and allow for them to be reused, teachers can use Velcro to stick the key vocabulary word cards onto the magnetic cards that come with the reader rather than brailling directly onto the magnetic cards.)

Students need to learn how to use the card reader to hear the words. This can take some time. Sometimes students also like to record the words, and enjoy hearing their own voices. When students are working independently with the cards and the card reader, they must remember to first read the word to themselves,

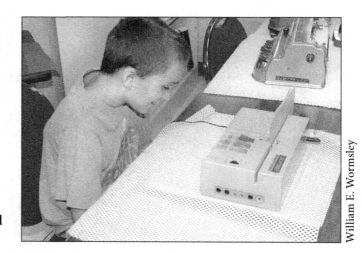

Student using a talking card reader.

and after reading it, they can then run it through the card reader to see if they read it correctly. The teacher should work with the child's classroom teacher to set up a station where the student can go to practice his or her words or phrases on a regular basis. The teacher can set up a routine where the student locates the words to practice and puts them in the "finished" basket when he or she has read them correctly.

RECORDKEEPING

Recordkeeping is extremely important when introducing and playing games with key vocabulary words. If the forms included in this practice guide (see Appendix) do not fit a teacher's organizational style, teachers can create their own forms, as long as they collect similar information.

Monthly Probes: Form for Recording Words Learned, Practice Dates, and Mastery

The teacher can use a data collection sheet such as the Form for Recording Words Learned, Practice Dates, and Mastery to track which words were introduced on which dates. An example of a completed form for a student named Ben appeared earlier in the chapter in Figure 4.1, and a blank version of the form is provided in the Appendix. This form provides space to record both key vocabulary words and filler words (see Chapter 7 for more on filler words).

When testing students on their word recognition, teachers should record whether the student read each word correctly or incorrectly on the date the student is tested. So, for example, if the teacher has introduced two words, and the student has practiced them to the point where the teacher is confident the student can identify them when mixed together, the teacher would create a test or game to assess the student's ability to do so. The teacher should strive for 100 percent accuracy with those two words before adding on additional words. The plus sign on the form indicates 100 percent accuracy.

Each month the teacher should do a probe of all the words the student has been introduced to up to that point to see which of the words the student is able to recognize. Consistent recognition of words at the monthly probes and when reading will be considered mastery. The Form for Recording Words Learned, Practice Dates, and Mastery provides a way of keeping track of what words the teacher has introduced, dates for when the words are practiced, and includes columns for the monthly probes.

As already noted, to be able to say that a student has mastered a word, the teacher must be able to demonstrate that the student continues to recognize the word over time. Sometimes a word that was recognized in one month is no longer recognized the next month, perhaps because it wasn't used as much or the student's interest in the word has waned. Teachers and their students may decide to keep using and testing a particular word that the student no longer remembers in order to maintain it in the child's reading vocabulary. In this case, the monthly probe should continue to include the word. As the I-M-ABLE approach moves into learning phonics and decoding, these words can be reintroduced and relearned by the student if necessary.

The Lesson Summary Sheet

The Lesson Summary Sheet (see Figure 4.2 and the Appendix) provides the teacher with a combination planning and recordkeeping tool. The form allows the teacher to document how much time is being spent with the student and on what types of activities. The form is flexible so that the teacher can indicate what was planned for a lesson and what was actually done—which might be completely different from the plan if the teacher takes advantage of a teachable moment. The form includes directions to explain how to use each of the four columns in the form.

Ben's teacher used this form to keep records of her daily lessons with him. Figure 4.2 shows a completed sample lesson plan using the Lesson Summary Sheet from one of her lessons with Ben. A blank Lesson Summary Sheet can be found in the Appendix.

The Lesson Summary Sheets can be kept in the student record book along with the Form for Recording Words Learned, Practice Dates, and Mastery.

FIGURE 4.2

Lesson Summary Sheet Filled Out for Ben

Directions for Using the Lesson Summary Sheet

This sheet is to be used for both planning and keeping records of what actually happened in the lesson.

Use one sheet per lesson. If more than one lesson takes place per day, use separate sheets for each.

<u>Complete</u> the top portion of the sheet with the student's name, date, and the individual who is working (or who is going to be working) with the student. Lesson start and end times should be filled in at the start and end of instruction. This will provide a running record of how much time is spent on lessons with the student.

Components

Underline the component or components that are planned for this lesson. Circle the ones actually worked on.

Plan for the Lesson

In this column, record the plan for the lesson, or, if providing guidance for another individual to work with the student, describe what he or she should plan to cover.

Instruction/Activities

This column should contain a description of what actually happened during the lesson. This may follow the plan closely or it might differ because a teachable moment presented an opportunity or because something extraneous occurred (a fire drill, for example, which can be both extraneous and a teachable moment).

Outcomes/Comments

In this column, record the outcomes of the lesson and include comments about child motivation, teacher motivation, or noteworthy happenings (such as things the student says, anecdotes, and the like).

Date: _11/15_   Time started: _9:30_

Student: _Ben_   Time ended: _10:30_

Instructor/other: _Ms. Kendrick_

Components	Plan for the Lesson What do you plan to do?	Instruction/Activities What did you actually do?	Outcomes/Comments
• Getting started • Key word introduction • (Word recognition) • (Tracking)	Review words with cards and 2 tracking stories	Read 5 word cards with no errors; Read 2 tracking stories: 1 with guiding stickers; 1 without guides	No errors; kept hands together on both stories; tracked across lines from beginning to end.

Components	Plan for the Lesson What do you plan to do?	Instruction/Activities What did you actually do?	Outcomes/ Comments
• (Reading stories) • (Writing stories) • Phonics • (Writing mechanics) • (Letter/contraction recognition) • Vocabulary • Comprehension • Other: ___	Test—through sorting cards—place one distractor in pile of "bumpy ball" cards	Gave student stack of bumpy ball cards with 1 "name" card	6/6 read correctly
	Read stack of known words with student	Didn't get to	
	Read—"I see the bumpy ball." sentences and story	Read story 2x	No errors. Remembered "the"
	Write sentences: help student write sentences using the words "bumpy ball."	Pulled actual ball out as Ben had difficulty figuring out what to say; gave language "bouncy" and "rolls away"; wrote (for student to read): The bumpy ball is bouncy. The bumpy ball rolls away.	ESL student—doesn't have a lot of expressive vocabulary. Writing sentences is giving him the words.

Video Recording Lessons

Periodically recording lessons on video provides the teacher a way to determine how much a student has progressed. Here are some suggestions of when a teacher may want to video record lessons:

- the first time a key vocabulary word or phrase is introduced to the student
- once a month, during a lesson, when new key vocabulary words or phrases are introduced
- when playing games
- when reading tracking stories, or reading "real" stories that the student and teacher have written
- when monthly word probes are conducted

Periodically compare the videotapes to help assess the progress the student is making.

INCORPORATING WRITING

How easily the teacher can incorporate writing into daily lessons depends on the student's writing skills. This may be the first time that a student has been introduced to writing, or the student may already be proficient in using the brailler. Students who have been using the brailler to write their name or letters may want to make their own word cards to take home and read to their parents. The teacher can encourage this and plan lessons around teaching the student how to use the brailler to do this. (Chapter 6 provides guidance on teaching a student how to use the brailler.)

The teacher can start with just one word, teaching the student how to spell the word and how to write it in braille. If the word contains a contraction, it may prompt a discussion of what letters are "hiding" in the contraction that will need to be written out completely. Writing the word in this way reinforces reading the word. The teacher will want to encourage the student to feel the word after he or she has written it in braille.

Students may use the Perkins Brailler, the Perkins SMART Brailler, or the Mountbatten for writing initially but should also have exposure to electronic braille notetakers. A good way to introduce students to a notetaker is to have them use the braille keyboard on the notetaker to write words they have recently learned to write using a brailler. For the first lesson, the teacher can set up the file for the student to store the key words. The student can then practice writing the words over and over again on the braille keyboard.

In a subsequent lesson, the teacher can teach the student how to turn on the notetaker and retrieve the file that was previously set up. Then the student can use speech to read what they previously wrote in the file, while following along on the refreshable braille display. After reading the word they wrote previously, the teacher can ask the student to choose another word with which to practice using the notetaker.

For students who have short attention spans, varying the activities can keep the student engaged and concentrating on learning to read and write. The next chapter discusses teaching tracking across multiple lines of braille by creating and reading tracking stories.

CHAPTER 5

Teaching Students to Track across Multiple Lines of Braille

Once students have learned the smooth tracking movements that were focused on when introducing the first key vocabulary words, as discussed in Chapter 4, the next step is to teach the students to apply these same movements in learning how to track and move from one line to the next on a page containing several lines of braille. This type of tracking is a necessary skill to have for reading stories. Rather than asking the students to track lines of braille without any meaning, I-M-ABLE encourages creating meaningful ways to teach how to track from one line to the next through the creation of "tracking stories."

CREATING TRACKING STORIES USING KEY VOCABULARY WORDS

Tracking needs to be meaningful in order for students to be engaged in the activity. Tracking multiple pages and lines of braille without any purpose other than to keep the fingers on the lines of the page does nothing to promote smooth tracking, since the student is not being asked to read anything. Teachers will notice that as soon as the activity involves actually reading something, the student's movements slow down and sometimes scrubbing occurs. For this reason, the I-M-ABLE approach to teaching tracking initially incorporates the key vocabulary words that students have already learned into very simple stories, often incorporating a game, that require students to practice tracking skills in order to enjoy the story. Even just one word can be enough to create an entire story.

Tracking stories have two parts:

1. a "story" or setup that the teacher will use to prompt the student to seek a known key vocabulary word

2. a page of braille that contains multiple lead-in and lead-out lines—similar to those used on flash cards—with the same key vocabulary word on each line

To create tracking stories, the teacher chooses a key vocabulary word that the student has already learned to recognize. The teacher comes up with a story or setup that will motivate the student to find the key vocabulary word. The teacher then prepares a page of braille where the key word appears one or more times within the lead-in and lead-out lines. For example, one teacher had a student whose key word was *Ridge*, the name of her dog. Ridge was always running away from the student, and so the "story" was that Ridge had run away and the student had to find Ridge in the lines of braille on the page. This gave the student the opportunity to learn how to track with a specific purpose. Telling a story around the key vocabulary word motivates the student to look for things in the lines of braille, and assures the teacher that students are not simply moving their fingers across the page but are moving them with the purpose of reading. Sidebar 5.1 provides directions for creating effective tracking stories.

Examples of Tracking Stories

Each of the following examples of tracking stories involves multiple lines with just one word (the key word) on each line. Although the examples may only show a line or two, it is best to fill the entire page, so that students track from the top of the page to the bottom across as many lines as possible. The teacher introduces the story to the student by telling him or her what the story is about and what word to look for.

Key Word: *pizza*. Two *l*'s represent the house and are placed at the right end of the line.

Teacher: The pizza boy has started out with our delivery. How far is he from our house? When you find the word *pizza*, you will know where he is. So when you see the word *pizza*, say *pizza* out loud. Keep moving across the line all the way to the end until you find the house. Those two tall lines at the end are our "house."

Key Word: *Bob* (student's name). Bob likes to swim.

Teacher: Bob is in the water at the pool. He has started swimming across to reach the other side. How far did he get? When you find *Bob*, say his name.

SIDEBAR 5.1

Creating Effective Tracking Stories to Teach Tracking on Multiple Lines

The goal of creating these tracking stories is to develop a short story or setup that will prompt the student to seek a known key word on the page of braille. The story should relate to the word's meaning for the student as much as possible.

- Think of activities the child enjoys or is familiar with, such as:
  - Swimming
  - Standing on stage (singing or performing)
  - Walking in the grass
  - Picking up Cheerios from the table
  - Waiting for pizza to be delivered
- Translate these activities into tracking exercises using known key words from the child's list of key words.
- Create a page of braille with the following guidelines:
  - Initially, use the key word or phrase only once on each line. Try to vary the position of the word from one line to the next.
  - The rest of the line should be filled with repeats of dots 2-5 unless there is a reason for using something else. For example, repeating the letter l (dots 1-2-3) for grass rather than dots 2-5 might make more sense. (The cells of dots 1-2-3 will represent stalks of grass, in which the key word can be found.)
  - Remember to include a space before and after each instance of the key word to separate it from the lead-in and lead-out lines.
  - Double or triple space between lines, and use the paper in a landscape orientation similar to children's reading books. (As children gain experience and demonstrate capability in tracking, you can decrease the line spacing from triple to double, and eventually to single spacing between lines.)
  - Initially, keep the lines all the same length and run them across the entire width of the page. Gradually decrease the length of some lines to give students practice with not missing shorter lines. Indented lines can also be included.
  - Use a nonslip material under the braille page so that the paper doesn't move. This is particularly important if the child is a one-handed reader.
  - Teach the child how to move his or her hands across the lines, keeping the four fingers of both hands together. Keep encouraging the student to use all four fingers of both hands unless he or she is physically unable to do so.
  - Initially, teach the child how to read to the end of one line, and then track back on that line to the beginning, before moving directly down to the next line. (More advanced methods of moving to the next line will be taught later.)

(continued on next page)

Helpful Hints

- Do not test students on word recognition when you are teaching tracking. Tell the student what word or phrase to expect to see, and then use the tracking exercises to teach tracking while at the same time reinforcing word recognition.
- As children learn letters, you can also develop tracking exercises that involve locating letters on the lines.
- Gradually, as children become more capable of tracking and can identify words, phrases, or letters, increase the difficulty of tracking stories or games to include more than one word, phrase, or letter on each line and use the tracking exercises as a way to incorporate word, phrase, or letter identification.
- As students begin to write stories using their key vocabulary words (see Chapter 7), the tracking skills they have developed will need to be applied to stories that don't have lead-in lines. Teachers need to be alert to determine if students are capable of tracking the stories without losing their place on the page before moving on to stories without lead-in lines.

Key Word: *Lady Gaga*

TEACHER: Lady Gaga is performing in concert. Find out whether she is on stage yet. When you find where she is on stage, say her name so I know you have found her. If she isn't there, let me know so I can go find her! [The line may or may not have the name *Lady Gaga* on it to indicate in some instances that she may not yet be on stage.]

Recordkeeping: Documenting Tracking Skills

The teacher will want to take periodic videos of the student reading to document progress in tracking braille. These videos can be compared to the baseline video the teacher took before tracking instruction began (see Chapter 2).

USING TRACKING STORIES TO TEACH STUDENTS HOW TO TRACK ACROSS A LINE AND MOVE TO THE NEXT

When introducing tracking initially, the task is just to have the student verify the word, *not* to recognize it. The goal of tracking is to have students learn how to move their hands efficiently from one line of braille to the next. Although the tracking stories initially consist of lines of all the same length, as students become more proficient in tracking, the lines should be modified to be of variable length. The system used for tracking, therefore, needs to include ways to make sure that lines are not missed.

The most effective way for students to learn to track is to move their hands together across the entire line to the end (from right to left) and then retrace that line with both hands together back to the beginning of the line. Once they reach the beginning of the line they have just tracked, they can move both hands together directly down to the next line and begin to track that line. Using this method ensures that they will not miss any lines. Eventually, students will begin to slide their fingers down while they are tracing the line back. Or they may even begin to use the left hand to track back while the right hand is still reading. Some teachers use very simple markers such as raised stars or shapes at the beginning or end of the lines to make sure students are tracking from the beginning to the ending of the line. When students gain proficiency with moving their hands on the lines, these markers can be removed.

Teachers can have students "ride" their hands initially when tracking to show what smooth tracking looks and feels like. (The students place their fingers over the teacher's as the teacher tracks across the line.) Eventually, the teacher can model the movements of smooth, efficient readers who separate their hands so that students know it is okay to do that. Students who are not explicitly told that it's okay and efficient to separate the hands may naturally learn to do so but only practice the technique in secret because they think their teacher will not approve.

A student reading a tracking story created for him.

Take the case of Amy. Amy's teacher started her reading with both hands together. As Amy got better at reading, she noticed that she was separating her hands when she was reading at home. However, Amy kept that a secret from her teacher and continued to use both hands together in school because that is what she thought her teacher wanted.

Though the primary goal of teaching tracking is to teach students how to move their hands and fingers, it is still a good idea for the teacher to ask the student to say the key word whenever he or she encounters it in a tracking story in order to reinforce word recognition. After tracking skills are well developed, these same types of tracking activities can be played with more than one word on a line, and word recognition can become the primary goal.

MOVING INTO READING ACTUAL STORIES

Smooth tracking skills are essential for students when they are reading real stories. The stories they read initially may have very short lines, so they need to be able to tell when they reach the end of the line and then move back across that line to the beginning and down to the next line. Once students are capable of reading words without the lead-in and lead-out lines, there is no longer a need to teach tracking using the tracking stories. The students can now use their tracking skills to read stories that they have written with their teachers (see Chapter 7), or even stories in books that are at their level of reading ability (see Chapter 10). However, the types of stories that were used to teach tracking can still be used to reinforce word recognition for new vocabulary words, or to have students play games to see what words, phrases, or letters are on a line. At that point, the goal of the tracking stories shifts from teaching tracking to assisting with word, phrase, or letter recognition or discrimination.

INCORPORATING WRITING

As mentioned at the beginning of this practice guide, each of the chapters presents a component of I-M-ABLE. There is no essential order in which to use these components, with the exception that the introduction of key vocabulary words is considered the starting point for the formal use of this approach.

The next chapter will introduce how to teach writing using the Perkins Brailler, another component of the approach. That chapter will provide information on ways to help students learn to write on the brailler, including creating their own tracking stories.

CHAPTER 6

Teaching Writing Mechanics in a Meaningful Way

The most commonly used tool for teaching writing in braille is the Perkins Brailler. Students need to become independent in using the brailler, which means they must eventually be able to know and do everything listed on the Mechanics of Using a Brailler form (see Figure 6.1).

There are several models of the Perkins Brailler available, including lighter touch versions, which don't require as much pressure to press down on the keys. One model has a paper support on the back, to make it easier to place the paper into the brailler, which can be especially useful for someone who may have limited use of his or her hands. The Perkins SMART Brailler speaks what is being brailled and displays it for the teacher or others on a screen. Perkins also sells extension keys for adapting braillers for students who may have additional physical difficulties affecting their hands and fingers that can prevent them from using the regular keys.

Other writing tools range from the slate and stylus to electronic notetakers with refreshable braille displays and stand-alone products such as the Mountbatten brailler. Introducing and teaching the use of more technological devices is not often considered an option for students with cognitive impairments who are struggling to read braille. However, electronic notetakers, with their refreshable braille displays, can generate excitement and motivation in students, who can see immediately what they have written as well as hear it voiced aloud. The Mountbatten brailler can produce the letter names as the student is writing and will also read the words. This can help reinforce correct fingering. Students should be exposed to as many writing tools as possible and be allowed to "scribble" on them and "create" stories in preparation for future writing experiences (for more information on teaching a beginning writer, see Swenson, 2016).

Eventually, students will need to learn how to fully operate the brailler, including how to load paper into it and take it out. The teacher will want to make a

FIGURE 6.1

Mechanics of Using a Brailler: Assessment and Sequence of Skills

	Recording Procedures: I = Skill introduced A = Skill achieved with assistance M = Skill achieved with mastery		
Skills	**I**	**A**	**M**
1. Identifies and uses the following parts of the brailler: embossing bar spacing keys backspacing key paper release levers paper feed knob embossing head lever line spacing key support bar feed roller left paper stop warning bell handle cover margin stop			
2. Operates brailler: Positions brailler correctly on work surface. Moves embossing head to correct positions. Rotates paper feed knob away from self. Pulls paper release levers all the way toward self. Holds paper against paper support with one hand and closes paper release with the other. Rolls paper into brailler until stopped by left paper stop. Depresses the line spacing key to lock paper position. Removes paper from the brailler. Leaves brailler in rest position when not in use (moves embossing head to the right as far as possible, leaves paper release lever open, and covers machine).			

Source: Reprinted from Wormsley, D. P., & D'Andrea, F. M. (Eds.). (1997). *Instructional strategies for braille literacy.* New York: AFB Press.

The APH light-touch Perkins Brailler.

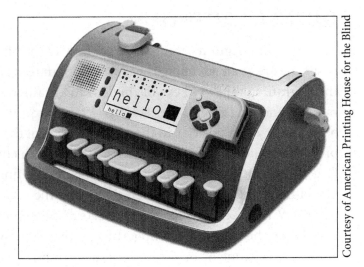

The APH SMART Brailler by Perkins.

student's first introduction to the brailler as much fun as possible and make use of the brailler meaningful to the student. For instance, rather than starting the student with the task of putting paper into the brailler, the teacher might put the paper in the brailler and then show a student who is new to using the Perkins Brailler the keys of the brailler and what fingers to use, so that he or she can begin to write something. Creating something to write is a lot more fun initially than learning about the equipment itself. Once students have had the opportunity to write something on the brailler, then the teacher can take some time to explore its parts with the student and begin to teach the skills needed for the student to become independent in its use.

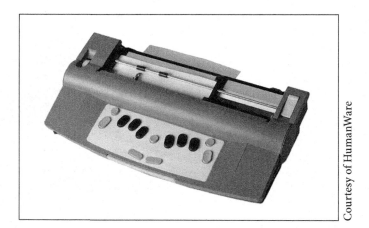

The Mountbatten brailler.

TEACHING CORRECT FINGERING

Teachers who begin teaching students how to use the keys of the brailler for the first time are at an advantage because they can teach correct fingering right from the beginning. The six keys of the Perkins Brailler permit the use of the index, middle, and ring fingers on each hand to create various braille letters and symbols. The keys are positioned three on each side of the space bar. The index fingers press down the keys closest to the space bar, which correspond to dot 1 (left index finger) and dot 4 (right index finger). The middle fingers press down keys corresponding to dot 2 (left) and dot 5 (right), and the ring fingers dot 3 (left) and dot 6 (right). When teaching a student to create a braille symbol, it is important to make sure he or she uses correct fingering on that symbol, and reinforce it with the student every time he or she brailles that symbol.

Students who are already brailling need to be assessed for how they use their fingers in producing braille on the Perkins Brailler. They may have developed all sorts of inefficient habits, such as using more than one finger to press down a key, or removing their fingers from the keys in between brailling one letter and the next, or simply not paying attention to which finger is correct and using any combination of fingers that they feel like. In order for students to become efficient braillers capable of accurately producing braille characters, they need to use the correct fingers on keys at all times. Those students who have not practiced correct fingering in the past may balk at having to relearn how to braille. Those who have not yet learned are ripe for beginning with the proper technique.

One of the best ways to teach the mechanics of writing is for the teacher to incorporate it into every lesson, if even for just a few moments. Involving another

Key configuration of the Perkins Brailler.

teacher or paraprofessional from the student's classroom in working on the mechanics of using the brailler can be helpful. Practice on the brailler can take place any time there is a lull in instruction, so having others able to reinforce what the student is learning permits the student much more practice with the braillewriter.

Students who have not used their hands very much may have difficulty initially with both their finger strength and dexterity. Poor finger strength or dexterity might result in students' not wanting to or not being able to initially use correct finger placement on the keys of the Perkins. Since any other devices that utilize a braille keyboard will use the same fingering, learning the correct fingering from the beginning is critical.

Motivation to learn to use the Perkins is greater if the materials being brailled are meaningful and interesting to the student doing the brailling. So while the task may be to strengthen the ring fingers on each hand, or to isolate the fingers so that the student can produce a particular character, the more interesting the activity is, the more likely it is that the student will persevere with the task. One student who had difficulty making the letter *x* was not very interested in simply making rows of *x*'s until his teacher connected the letter *x* to one of his key words, which was *train*. The teacher told the student that he had to make the tracks for the train to travel on. At that point, making rows of *x*'s became a fun activity that the student happily engaged in, making comments when he made a mistake about the train derailing and laughing about his tracks when they weren't quite correct. Needless to say, he was more adept at using his fingers to braille the letter *x* after a few sessions of making train tracks!

As important as it is for students to use correct fingering for a letter, it is just as important to be sure they are moving from one letter to another in a smooth transition. Just as in touch typing, the fingers should be placed on the proper keys and should stay in contact with or just above those keys when they are not in use. To make the letter *a*, only finger 1 (left index finger) is pressed down, while the other fingers rest lightly on the other keys, or lift up just slightly. If a student gets into the habit of removing the fingers that are not in use and curling them under, then those fingers are not ready to be used for the next character to be brailled. When students curl their fingers under in this way, they consistently lose the reference of where their fingers belong, and constantly have to reposition their fingers. Curling unused fingers is, therefore, not an efficient method of writing braille. Part of the initial practice that teachers should comment on is how well students keep their fingers in contact with the appropriate keys on the brailler.

Some students who have trouble with finger strength may try using two fingers to press down a key. This practice makes it more likely that at some point the student will braille some letters inaccurately, since one of those fingers has to come off the key for which it is supposed to be used in order to "help" the other finger. It is particularly problematic when a student removes his or her index finger from the key for either dot 1 or dot 4 and uses it and the middle finger to press down the key for dots 2, 3 5, or 6. Teachers will want to encourage the students to make every finger strong! Some teachers have created "garages" using curved bits of cardboard around each key, or Velcro taped to each key, so that only one finger can fit into the "garage."

Once students have some confidence in their ability to use the keys of the Perkins Brailler, teachers can help them learn the everyday mechanics of use, such as line spacing and putting paper in and taking it out. Students will have a more satisfactory experience if the teacher models how to put the paper in and lets the students feel where to place their hands for various tasks. Then the teacher can let the students explore what happens when they press the different keys, such as the line space key and the backspace key, and use the embossing head return. Using a teaching technique such as backward chaining can be helpful with students who have cognitive impairments. In backward chaining, the steps for learning to do a task are listed in order and teaching begins with the last step first. In this way, the student always experiences the success of completing the task. For example, the teacher may perform all of the steps in Figure 6.2 up to pressing the line space key. Then he or she would ask the student to slide the embossing head back to the beginning of the line in preparation for writing. The student and teacher can then work on some of the writing exercises mentioned earlier. When the student finishes writing, the teacher may teach the student how to remove paper from the brailler (Figure 6.2). Gradually, the other steps are taught in order from last to first and eventually the student can insert the paper, write on the brailler, and remove the paper independently.

FIGURE 6.2

Steps for Loading and Removing Paper from a Brailler

Steps for Loading Paper into the Brailler	
Step	Date Mastered
1. Roll the paper feed knobs backward (away from you) until they stop.	
2. Pull the paper release levers forward (toward you).	
3. Hold the paper with the holes on the left side.	
4. Lay the paper flat on the paper support bar or reading rest.	
5. Slide the paper under the embossing head (centered).	
6. Slide the paper all the way to the left.	
7. Push the paper release levers back.	
8. Roll the paper in.	
9. Press the line-spacing key once.	
10. Slide the embossing head all the way to the left.	
Steps for Removing Paper from the Brailler	
Step	Date Mastered
1. Roll the paper feed knobs backward (away from you) until they stop.	
2. Pull the paper release levers forward (toward you).	
3. Grasp the paper and remove it from the brailler.	

Source: Adapted from Swenson, A. M. (2016). *Beginning with braille: Firsthand experiences with a balanced approach to literacy* (2nd ed., p. 20). New York: AFB Press.

INCORPORATING WRITING INTO LESSONS

Writing doesn't have to wait until students have amassed a list of vocabulary words. Teaching students how to use the brailler for writing can be incorporated into many early lessons such as the learning of key vocabulary words. Students can learn to write the initial letters of their key words or the wordsigns and groupsigns that make up various contractions in their key words. One student was enamored with the *in* sign, which she had learned from the name of Linkin Park, a rock band. She talked about the feel of the *in* sign and asked for more words that used the *in* sign. Her teacher had her braille some rows of the *in* sign, and she was also able to use it with several initial consonants that she had already learned to write, to form the words *pin*, *fin*, and *kin*. Thus, a reading lesson became a writing lesson, which in turn became a phonics lesson. This is a good demonstration of how the various components of I-M-ABLE can be used simultaneously to reinforce each other.

BRAILLING TRACKING STORIES

Students may also enjoy creating their own tracking stories, like the examples provided in Chapter 5. The teacher can give students a chance to recreate a story that they had previously read, and then encourage them to try to think of one on their own. This can be a separate lesson, or one that the student does with a paraprofessional or at home. If the student does this at home, either the student or his or her parents will need to know how to load the paper into the brailler and how to create the lead-in and lead-out lines as well as write the word to be used in the tracking story.

Teachers can help students think of a tracking story that they can write. It is sometimes hard for students to think of these stories; indeed, it is hard for teachers also! Don't worry if the story doesn't make a whole lot of sense or if it is a repeat of one that has already been done with the student. The goal is to have students use the brailler for writing.

Tips for Brailling Tracking Stories

The following are some points to remember when working with students on brailling tracking stories:

- Make sure that students are using the correct fingers on the keys, even when just writing the lead-in or lead-out lines.
- Make sure that students leave a space before and after the words they write.
- Make sure that students double or triple space the lines according to what will best enable them to read the story.

Brailling Drawings

Writing can also be related to the key words in other ways. One student loved NASCAR auto racing—it was one of his key vocabulary words. To help him strengthen his fingers, his paraprofessional created a simple drawing of a car that he could make on the brailler by following her directions. The drawing involved creating certain letters and contractions in a certain order, which helped him with his finger strength and finger positioning on the keys. He was very proud of his drawings and loved giving them to others after they were made!

Charlson (2010) has created a book of 36 drawings that can be made by students using the Perkins Brailler; teachers can also make their own drawings by tracing a simple shape on graph paper, determining which braille characters would best represent the shape, and whether it should be filled in or open.

READING THEIR WRITING

When print readers are learning to write, it is not possible to separate the task of writing and reading. Print readers get to see and read the letter they are writing as they are writing it. Using the Perkins Brailler requires both hands on the keys, which doesn't permit the student to read what he or she is writing as he or she is writing it. The Perkins SMART Brailler or the Mountbatten brailler, which provide audio feedback, are good in that the student receives reinforcement that he or she formed the correct letter, but hearing what was written doesn't replace the reading of the letter itself. When teaching writing, the teacher will want to encourage students to reach up from the keys to the paper so they can feel what they have written. Students need to get into the habit of examining their efforts, while at the same time not doing this so often that they are constantly losing their place on the braille keys.

Students who are beginning to learn how to write might need to reach up and feel after every letter, and then after every word. Eventually, a good stopping point will be when a student moves from one line down to the next, whether what was produced was a whole line of full cells, or a line of letters that a student is practicing, or a spelling word that contained the contraction *in*, or a sentence in a story that the student is writing.

Writing can reinforce students' progress in reading. Students will eventually move from whole word recognition to recognizing letters at the beginnings of words, including contractions. Writing these letters and practicing them can reinforce the feel of the letters (especially since the teacher will ask the student to read what he or she has written.) As students learn to write more and more letters, they can begin to write the key vocabulary words that they know and also begin to write some short phrases. Eventually they will move into sentences and short stories using the words that they know. When students are at the point where they are learning to recognize words using onset/rime—the initial sounds of a word and word family endings, further discussed in Chapter 8—then the writing can include activities relating to writing the words that the student has learned to recognize. The goal is independent use of the Perkins Brailler and any other equipment that the student uses for writing. Getting to that goal requires daily work in writing as well as reading.

RECORDKEEPING

The Mechanics of Using a Brailler in Figure 6.1 can be used by teachers to keep track of what a student is doing and when he or she has mastered the various steps. In addition, the teacher can keep notes on how well the student uses his or her fingers on the brailler. To keep track of the letters and contractions that the student knows how to write, the teacher can simply highlight what the student knows on one of the many braille cheat sheets that exist. The cheat sheet will also help anyone who is helping the student with the correct braille configurations (although it might not help with the rules of when to use them!).

COLLABORATING WITH OTHERS

Other people can help the student with his or her writing as long as they know how to use the braillewriter and what the student is capable of doing independently. To help others work with the student, the teacher can photocopy the Mechanics of Using a Brailler form from the Appendix and write the student's name and the words "is able to" at the top. If a teacher has been using the form in his or her recordkeeping, the teacher may simply copy that form, with the various boxes filled in, so that the student's helper knows what he or she has mastered. The individual working with the student will also need to know everything that is on this form, so it might be helpful to have a picture of the brailler with the various parts identified close by (see Figure 6.3). Also, since the teacher, parent, or paraeducator who will be helping needs to know how to use the brailler, it is a good opportunity to provide a hands-on demonstration for those people as a group. Post the form nearby to where the student uses the Perkins Brailler in the classroom or at home, so that whoever works with the student will see what he or she can do independently and will encourage the student to continue practicing.

The teacher can demonstrate for those who are working with the student the proper way to keep the fingers in position when brailling so that they can reinforce this when they are working with the student. Also, the teacher can provide a picture showing a student's fingers on the keys in the proper positions, as well as what *not* to allow students to do with their hands.

FIGURE 6.3

Parts of the Braillewriter

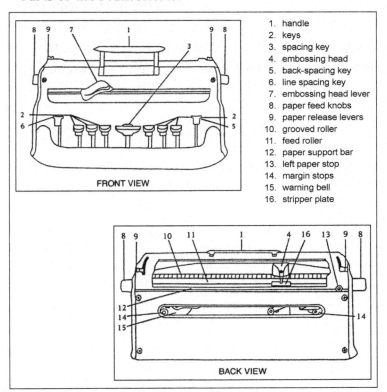

Source: Reprinted with permission from Stratton, J. M., & Wright, S. (2010). *On the way to literacy: Early experiences for visually impaired children* (p. 344). Louisville, KY: American Printing House for the Blind.

Proper hand and finger positions on the keys of the Perkins Brailler.

William E. Wormsley

Expanding the capability of students to write will allow for use of these physical writing skills when collaborating with the teacher to create stories which the student writes and then can read, as discussed in Chapter 7. Initially the teacher may demonstrate the writing for the student, and then urge the student to take over more and more of that writing as they continue developing the student's story.

CHAPTER 7

Collaborating with Students to Create Key Vocabulary Stories

Talking with students about their key vocabulary words or phrases leads to learning more about what the student is interested in. These discussions often lead into the development of stories and the identification of additional key vocabulary words. As the teacher talks with the student, the teacher will want to take notes on the discussion and keep track of any new key vocabulary words the student might want to learn, as well as the topics that might make for good stories.

These stories will be similar to the stories that the teacher might have created for students about their own experiences (see Chapter 2), with the exception that those earlier stories were designed to be read to students and to expose them to written language in the form of braille, while the stories that the teacher will write here are designed for students to read themselves, and will therefore initially be simpler and more repetitive.

FIRST COLLABORATIVE STORIES

Ideally, the first stories the teacher and the student write together will include a key vocabulary word or words that the student has been learning, and will also need to include some other filler words—words that are not familiar to the student but are needed in order to create a story.

While the teacher talks with the student, the teacher should take out the brailler. When the student says something that might be part of a story, the teacher can indicate that this would make a good story to read, and can begin to write on the brailler what the student is saying. The teacher will want to leave room at the top for a title that will be agreed upon when the story is finished.

Sometimes these early stories will involve the student; sometimes they will involve others who are important to the student such as his or her friends, family, or pets. Since the teacher is taking the lead from the student, let the student dictate what he or she wants to have in the story. Five or six sentences on a page should be enough to begin a story. A student's first story might be as simple as the following:

> I like **pizza**.
> I like **Lady Gaga**.
> I like **pizza** and **Lady Gaga**.

While *pizza* and *Lady Gaga* are the student's key vocabulary words, the phrase *I like* is not but was needed to make the key vocabulary words into stories. Thus, it is a filler phrase.

Stories like this often lead to the learning of other words. After writing this story, the student's teacher developed a phrase card for *I like* so that the student could learn the new phrase. The teacher introduced the phrase card the next time the two had a lesson and reminded the student that this phrase had started the story written in the last lesson. They explored the features in the phrase *I like* in the same way they explored a new key vocabulary word, looking for tactilely significant features. The capital dot in front of *I* and the use of the whole word contraction for *like,* with the space in between the two, made the phrase an easy one to remember and to distinguish from other key vocabulary words.

Introducing a phrase such as *I like* can lead to discussion of what else the student likes. So a simple story can lead to more words, which can be added to the story, thus creating a longer story.

Language Experience Stories

Another way to create stories with students is to use the *language experience approach*, in which the student creates a story about an experience he or she has had. This is generally best done after something significant has occurred that the student wants to talk about. Sometimes a field trip to a favorite spot can trigger the story; other times it can be something that happened in the classroom or at home. The steps in the language experience approach (Leu & Kinzer, 1991) include:

- Participating in an experience that will provide content for a story.
- Having students describe the experience in their own words.

- Assisting students in creating a story (usually as a group, but this can work with individual students also).
- Writing that story on a chart (or brailling it on a brailler).
- Helping students read what has been written.

The teacher establishes with the student that they will write a story together about the experience. Then the teacher lets the student talk about what he or she wants to say, in his or her own words. While some advocate keeping grammatical errors intact in the story, it can also benefit a student to hear what the correct English would be. For example, a student may say, "We all happy" instead of "We are all happy." The teacher can say, "That's right! We are all happy," and insert the correct words. Or a student might say, "He be green." And the teacher can again say something similar like, "Yes, he IS green, isn't he?" This way of "correcting" the student is respectful and responsive, in that it allows the student to see the difference in what he or she said and what the teacher said, while at the same time acknowledging that the student had the meaning or concept correct. Then the teacher writes the sentence with the correct grammar in the story so that the student will read the sentence multiple times, thus reinforcing the correct grammatical structure.

In using the language experience approach, the teacher models writing the story in braille, and then models reading the story after it is finished while the student reads along on the braille copy that the teacher created.

Using Real Objects

The teacher will want to be alert to using real objects with students when necessary or even to enhance the learning of the story. One student had the word *purse* as one of her key words. Her teacher brought in a purse for them to talk about. In talking about the purse, the student wanted to know where the keys were and where the cell phone was. Suddenly there were two new key vocabulary words: *keys* and *cell phone*. The teacher brought in a set of old keys and an old cell phone for the purse the next day. Then *lotion* became a talking point, and soon the purse had lotion in it. The story they created read something like the following:

>I have a **purse**.
>I have **keys** in my **purse**.
>I have a **cell phone** in my **purse**.
>I have **lotion** in my **purse**.

I like my **purse**.
I like my **keys**.
I like my **cell phone**.
I like my **lotion**.

Another student, Hannah (mentioned in Chapter 1), wrote many such stories with her teacher, including a humorous story entitled *The Poo Book*, which Hannah and her teacher wrote together after a visit to a farm where they encountered *poo*. Hannah insisted that they use as many of her key words as possible, which are highlighted in the following story.

The **Poo** Book
Poo poo poo.
A **horse** can **poo**.
A **cow** can **poo**.
Chickens can **poo**.
A **rat** can **poo**.
A **dinosaur** can **poo**.
A **baby** can **poo**.
A **grandma** can **poo**.
A **grandpa** can **poo**.
A **mummy** can **poo**.
A **daddy** can **poo**.
Hannah can **poo**.
Can you **poo** too?

Points to Consider When Writing Stories with Students

When writing stories with students, keep the following suggestions in mind:

- Use punctuation and capital dots for capital letters. Don't make the punctuation too complicated in the beginning. Periods at the ends of sentences and possibly exclamation points are enough to begin with for the student to get a good sense of them.
- Write the stories on paper that is 8.5 by 11, with the paper inserted the wide way initially.
- Double space between lines.
- Let the discussion around writing the story help the student develop a deeper understanding of the meanings of the words he or she is using. (A child may be fascinated by a word but not really have an understanding of what it is. The discussions will maintain his or her interest and also teach the full meaning of the word.)

- When possible, use the stories to expand the student's language base.
- Writing the story on a brailler as the child dictates it is a way of modeling braille writing for a student who may not have heard others writing braille. It may also lead to interest in the brailler and in writing.

READING THE STORIES

The stories the student writes with the teacher can be collected and put into a booklet. As the stories grow in number, students can practice reading them and can take the booklet home to be read to their parents, siblings, and other relatives. The teacher will also want to keep copies of the stories in the student record book in case anything happens to the student's booklet. These stories can also be read to others in the classroom. One student had a story that he practiced over and over. He finally asked his three buddies in the resource room if they wanted to hear his story. The story was about camping. The three buddies lined up their chairs in a circle around the student, and he read the story to them. When he finished, they applauded him and told him to give them "high fives." His teacher reported that the expression on his face when his classmates "high fived" him was one of pure joy and pride!

These early stories will most likely have a great deal of repetition, which reinforces the reading. Words that are needed for sentences to develop meaning can become words a student wants to learn just because they occur in meaningful sentences. The teacher can create word cards for these words, thus increasing the reading vocabulary for the student.

Sample Stories

Following are examples of other stories that have been written with students:

> Mike's **Money** Book
> Mike likes **money.**
> Mike likes a **penny.**
> Mike likes more **pennies.**
> Mike likes a **nickel.**
> Mike likes more **nickels.**
> Mike likes a **dime.**
> Mike likes more **dimes.**
> Mike likes a **quarter.**
> Mike likes more **quarters.**
> Mike likes **money.**

Making **Popcorn**
    Put the **popcorn** in the **popper**.
    Turn it on, turn it on.
    Pop, pop, pop, pop,
    Pop, pop, pop.
    When the **popping** stops,
    Now that's the best part.
    We all eat **popcorn** and we cannot stop!
    Pop, pop, pop, pop,
    Pop, pop, pop.

What We **Like**
    Maria likes **swimming**.
    Jill likes **roller skating**.
    Jen likes **bowling**.
    We all like **eating!**

    Maria went to the **grocery store**.
    Jill went to the **grocery store**.
    Jen went to the **grocery store**.
    We all went to the **grocery store!**

    Maria and **Jill** like **bowling**.
    Maria and **Jill** like **shopping**.
    Maria and **Jill** like **school**.
    Maria and **Jill** like the **gym**.
    Maria and **Jill** like **Jen**.
    Maria and **Jill** like **Mrs. B**.
    Maria and **Jill** like having fun!

    Maria came to school on the **bus**.
    Maria said **hello**.
    Jill came to school on the **bus**.
    Jill said **hello**.
    Jen came to school on the **bus**.
    Jen said **hello**.
    Mrs. B said **hello** to **Maria**.
    Mrs. B. said **hello** to **Jill**.
    Mrs. B. said **hello** to **Jen**.
    We all said **hello**.

Valentine's Day
    I like **Valentine's Day**.
    Mommy likes **Valentine's Day**.

> **Mommy** and I like **Valentine's Day.**
> We all like **Valentine's Day!**

These stories are more sophisticated than the original stories created during the early literacy phase, and they all incorporate repetition to a greater or lesser extent. They also include more and more filler words, as the students are not so tied to learning just their key vocabulary words. Teachers should create and teach word cards for the phrases and the words included in these stories to demonstrate to students how their reading vocabulary is growing, and to determine if they can read the words in isolation from the story. These words and phrases can be introduced either before or after reading the story, but at some point teachers should examine them with the students in the same way the key vocabulary words were examined—talking about how they feel to the touch. Since by the time students are reading and writing stories like this they will probably also have learned some letters or contractions, teachers can discuss the initial letters with them as well and let students comment as to whether they recognize any other letters or contractions in the words.

Points to Consider When Reading Stories Written with Students

When reading stories, keep the following suggestions in mind:

- Once the story is created, don't expect the student to be able to read it immediately. Read the story to the student as he or she follows along. Pause periodically when expecting the student to be able to read a word, and allow the student time to read it. If the student doesn't read the word, then the teacher can say it for him or her.
- As the student learns the story, the teacher and the student can take turns reading lines. The teacher reads one; the student reads the next one; and so on.
- Interline or make a print copy of the story for others who do not know braille to read with the student.
- Encourage the student to read the story to others.
- Have the student reread the story often to reinforce word recognition and to increase reading fluency.
- Have the student pick a story to "publish" as a separate book. That way he or she can learn about pages, covers, binding, illustrations, and the like. The student can decorate the cover and create tactile illustrations for the pages of the book.

GAMES AND ACTIVITIES WITH KEY VOCABULARY STORIES

Cut-Apart Stories

Once there are stories written that the student is able to read, the sentences can be cut apart into sentence strips. Students can then practice reading the sentences separately. If the story has a sequence, the teacher can ask the student to put the sentence strips in the right order.

The teacher can also use these sentences and paste them onto the magnetic talking card reader cards for practice reading. The teacher can ask the student to read the sentence, and then run it through the card reader to see if he or she is correct.

Audio Recorded Stories

Students enjoy hearing themselves on an audio recording. The teacher can ask the student to pick one of his or her stories to read out loud. This can be a motivator for practicing fluency prior to the recording. Then the teacher can record the student reading the story and play it back while they both read along in the story.

Magnetic Word Board

The teacher can use Brailon (a plastic-like paper sold by specialty vendors; see the Resources section at the back of this book) to put individual braille words onto magnets. The words can then be moved around on a magnetic board or a cookie tray to create some funny stories. Students can read the words they have selected as if they are a poem, or try to see if the words make them think of stories they might write. This is similar to the magnetic poetry kits that one finds in bookstores.

Writing Sentences

The teacher can help the student select a sentence from one of his or her stories to learn to write. As the teacher helps the student write the sentence, he or she will want to make sure that the student knows where capital dots and punctuation are needed. The teacher can also discuss what writing a sentence involves, such as spacing between words, punctuation at the end, and a capital letter at the beginning, and have the student find these elements as he or she reads the sentence.

Incorporating Technology

Just as a braille notetaker can be incorporated into writing when the student is learning to write key vocabulary words (see Chapter 4), a notetaker can be incor-

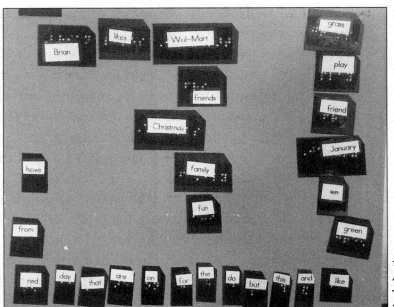

A teacher-made magnetic word board.

porated into writing sentences. The teacher can set up a file for sentences in the same way that he or she set up a file for words. Or, perhaps the student may be ready to learn how to set up the file him- or herself. The teacher can use a "think aloud" approach, speaking out loud the steps he or she is taking to set up the file in order to model the task for the student. Once the student has written a sentence on the Perkins Brailler, the teacher can ask him or her to write the same or a different sentence on the notetaker and then have the student learn how to read back the sentence.

Tips for Helping Students Write Their Own Stories

Students will initially need a lot of help when learning to write their own stories, especially if they are still becoming familiar with the brailler or notetaker. Often, students who have additional cognitive disabilities have a hard time when confronted with the task of writing an entire story. Here are some suggestions for getting students ready to write a story of their own. These steps may take several lessons to accomplish.

- Model writing a story for the student.
  - Talk about how you get your ideas, how you decided what you are going to write about. Make the story something that will be interesting to the student so that he or she will want to read the story when it is finished. Use

some of the student's own key or filler words so that it reinforces his or her reading of those words.
- Keep the story simple the first time. It should be less than a page, but it can be several sentences. The idea is to let the student know that stories don't have to have the repetition that was in the stories the teacher and student wrote previously to promote the student's reading. As the teacher writes the sentences, he or she should talk out loud about what he or she is thinking about, such as how to put in a capital dot or how to spell the words or include contractions.
- When the story is finished, let the student follow along while the teacher reads it. The student should have the braille copy while the teacher reads from another print or braille copy he or she has made.

- Talk with the student about what he or she might want to write a story about. Getting ideas is sometimes difficult. Help the student think about things he or she likes.
- Once the student has determined a topic, ask him or her to convey exactly what he or she wants to write.
  - Write what he or she says on the Perkins Brailler so the student hears you writing. This is similar to the process for developing stories using the language experience approach, except that this time the purpose is to have the student think about this as creative writing.
  - Help the student read the stories he or she wrote.
  - Take each sentence and have the student write the sentence on the brailler one at a time.
  - Have the student read the story.
- Repeat the steps above with the student for a number of stories, but begin to ask the student to take over more and more of the initial writing.
- When the student has no difficulty coming up with topics and thinking of things to write, audio record the student while he or she is telling the story. Then allow the student to listen to the story and stop the recording periodically in order to write down what he or she dictated, with the teacher's help if necessary.
- Often students write stories that are modeled after stories they have heard. Chapter 2 and the Resources section include a list of the types of predictable stories that were suggested for reading to children. The teacher might find some stories that will interest his or her student and suggest that others read them to the student. Even older students enjoy being read to. When the topic of the story is of interest to the student, rest assured that he or she will want

to have someone read it aloud. Reading about topics of interest provides students with new models of what stories sound like in addition to the ones they have written, and gives them additional vocabulary to use in creating their own stories about the topic.

RECORDKEEPING

In addition to collecting the stories that the student writes and learns to read, the teacher will want to keep anecdotal comments about the difficulty of the process for the student in the student record book. This permits the teacher to determine how the student is progressing on the way to becoming an independent writer of his or her own stories.

Creating stories such as these will also make teachers more aware of the various interests their students have. The discussion around the choice of a topic will enlighten the teacher as to the things that are important to the student. Teachers will want to make a note of these important topics or interests for future reference, especially when it's time to expand the student's vocabulary. The teacher may also want to use these interests to locate some small, commercially made reading books for the student, as discussed in Chapter 9.

As teachers implement each of the components of I-M-ABLE to this point, they may find their students interested in specific letters in words, or specific contractions. If teachers have been following the principles of I-M-ABLE, it is likely they have used that interest to teach those letters or contractions, and have pointed out to students the sounds that these letters and contractions make in words. This incidental teaching of phonics needs to be addressed in a more systematic way, however, if students are going to be able to move ahead in reading. Chapter 8 addresses learning letters, contractions, and teaching phonics to students as a systematic part of using the I-M-ABLE approach.

CHAPTER 8

Using Key Vocabulary Words to Teach Phonics, Letter Recognition, and Contractions

While I-M-ABLE begins with teaching whole words, it also provides for instruction in phonics. I-M-ABLE uses a student's key vocabulary words as starting points for phonics instruction, and incorporates the letters in these key vocabulary words into activities for letter recognition and contraction recognition.

Several researchers have suggested that students who have difficulty learning to read may find it easier to learn letters, contractions, and their sounds when they are related to words that have meaning for them and that they already know how to pronounce (Millar, 1997; Moustafa, 1997). I-M-ABLE is what Moustafa (1997) refers to as an analytic (or whole-to-part) approach to phonics instruction, where students are taught a number of sight words (words that students learn to recognize by sight as whole words, rather than by decoding) and then are taught to generalize from those words to other words. I-M-ABLE is also analogy-based instruction in that it teaches letter patterns that can be learned from analyzing the key vocabulary words, and then applied (by analogy) to unfamiliar words that have the same patterns. How I-M-ABLE differs from traditional whole-to-part phonics teaching is that in this approach the equivalent of sight words are meaningful key vocabulary words that will be different for each student. Therefore, the initial phonics lessons will differ from student to student also.

PHASES IN TEACHING PHONICS

Key vocabulary words used in teaching phonics and letter and contraction recognition follow the developmental phases for learning to read words: pre-alphabetic, partial alphabetic, full alphabetic, and consolidated alphabetic (Gaskins, Ehri, Cress, O'Hara, & Donnelly, 1997).

Pre-Alphabetic Phase

The *pre-alphabetic phase* is referred to (for print readers) as the "logographic" or "visual cue" phase (Vacca et al., 2012). In this phase words are recognized by some outstanding visual feature, such as the golden arches for the *M* in McDonald's. The preponderance of environmental print for preschoolers to learn from is the impetus for creating a braille-rich environment for young children with visual impairments, such as that mentioned in Chapter 2. This phase is where I-M-ABLE begins as an approach, presenting whole words or phrases and pointing out to students the distinctive, tactile features of the word that will help them remember the word and distinguish it from other words. In braille this can be called the *tactile cue* phase. Coupled with the fact that the words being taught are meaningful key vocabulary words, using whole words allows students to feel successful at reading and allows them to develop their tactile abilities and language of touch in relation to those meaningful words.

As students learn more and more words, however, it becomes harder to find tactilely distinct features that are significantly different from each other without beginning to talk about the individual characters (the letters or contractions) themselves. When whole words that are recognized in a pre-alphabetic way become too much to handle, I-M-ABLE begins to formally introduce letter recognition, which may or may not have already been touched upon by teacher and student. Moving students into the partial alphabetic phase will help increase their word-recognition capability.

Partial Alphabetic Phase

In the *partial alphabetic phase*, print-reading students make some connections between letters and sounds. They may remember that the letter *b* looks like a bat with a ball after it and that it makes the sound /b/, which begins both of those words. Word recognition does not resemble full decoding but rather involves the use of initial letter sounds to assist with remembering the word, and perhaps using an ending letter as well.

In I-M-ABLE, when students begin to identify or learn the initial letters of their key vocabulary words, they begin to move into the partial alphabetic phase of reading. They will start to learn to recognize individual letters by their tactile characteristics and will begin to learn to recognize a word by one or more letters in the word. Sometimes the discussion of letters comes out of a teachable moment within a lesson. The student may have two words that begin with the same letter. Thus, the first letter or shape is no longer going to be a distinguishing identifying feature. So the teacher names the letter and its sound, and then teacher and student discuss the two words that begin with that letter (and sound) and also pick other features of the two words that will help distinguish them from each other.

For example, the word *beautiful*, which may have been recognized because it was long, may be followed by another word beginning with *b*, such as *bird*. This is a prime opportunity for pointing out that *bird* begins the same way *beautiful* does, and that the sound of the letter at the beginning is the same. Learning about *b* in this way makes it more meaningful because it is connected to two words that are meaningful. *Beautiful* is longer and has an *l* at the end, and *bird* is shorter with no *l*. Both letters *b* and *l* now have more meaning to the student as a result of the word associations.

In other instances, the teacher may simply point out the letter at the beginning of the word and talk with the student about that letter, its name, its sound, what it feels like, and how to remember how to recognize that letter. Teachers do need to spend some time analyzing the differences between the letters in braille. Print-reading students use visualization of what the letters look like—for example, *o* is a circle like what your mouth looks like when you say "oh"; *s* looks like a snake which makes the sound /ssssss/; or *i* has a dot at the top. Braille doesn't lend itself to these same types of analogies, so students may simply need to memorize the configuration of the letter.

Teachers may use enlarged tactile letters formed with tools such as the Swing Cell or the Pop-A-Cell, available from American Printing House for the Blind. The Swing Cell consists of two wooden blocks, joined together at the top, with three holes drilled in each block so there are two rows of three holes. Pegs can be inserted into these holes to resemble the dots in the braille cell. A hinge at the top permits the two blocks to swing open, which is how it gets its name. When it is open, the dots correspond to the six keys on the brailler, and students can place their fingers on the pegs to see which keys of the brailler they must press down to get the same character they just felt when the Swing Cell was closed. The Pop-A-Cell

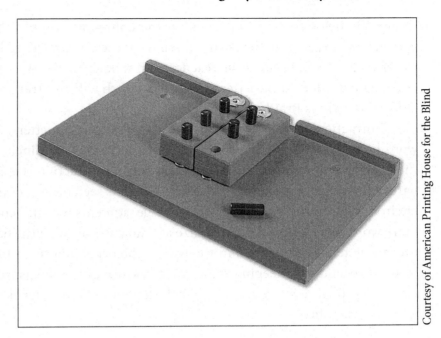

The Swing Cell in its closed position.

The Pop-A-Cell.

is smaller than the Swing Cell, and allows for the user to "pop" or depress the cells which aren't in use in the braille configuration. They can then be "popped" back to create the full cell.

Both the Swing Cell and the Pop-A-Cell allow the configuration of the braille cell to be enlarged over what a student would feel with regular braille. Enlarging the braille helps the student focus on the configuration, but the information gained from examining the enlarged cell must then be translated back down into the size of the real braille cell. Teachers can talk about the two columns of dots and where the dots in the letter are located, which will also transfer to writing on either the Perkins Brailler or the slate.

Contractions can be taught in the same manner as letters. Sometimes the word begins or ends with a contraction, or there is a prominent contraction in the word that the student has noted. Learning a contraction is really no easier or harder than learning a letter to a student who has seen little of either in his or her environment. In the partial alphabetic stage, students will still continue to learn more words which they will recognize as whole words, with the help of a few significant letters or characters in the words, thus enabling them to increase their reading vocabulary. Keeping these words meaningful will ensure motivation to read and provide a reference point for the letters and characters to assist students with learning them.

Full Alphabetic Phase

The partial alphabetic phase is gradually replaced by the *full alphabetic phase*. Print readers enter this phase when they have learned all of the letters and their sounds and can begin to figure out unfamiliar words by sounding out letters and blending them into sounds. Because of their exposure to environmental print, print readers move fairly quickly into this phase of reading. The partial alphabetic phase is also where traditional approaches place the emphasis in teaching beginning braille reading.

As students move through the partial alphabetic phase, I-M-ABLE concentrates more and more on moving students to the full alphabetic phase through the introduction of activities to help students recognize letters and sounds. As students learn to recognize more and more vocabulary words, they will learn more and more letters and contractions. Some of this learning will occur as a result of the choice of the words the students make for learning. However, teachers will need to ensure that students are making progress toward the full alphabetic phase in which students are able to identify the sounds for all letters and, in the case of braille, all contractions. If the words learned up to this point do not provide opportunities for learning new letters and contractions, the teacher will need to construct learning situations for students that will introduce them to the letters and contractions not currently found in the words they are learning.

Consolidated Alphabet Phase

The *consolidated alphabet phase* is generally considered to follow the full alphabetic phase of development. In the consolidated alphabet phase students are able to divide words into onsets and rimes (such as in the word *m-at* or *c-at*). *Onsets* are the initial sounds of a word, and *rimes* are the word family endings, often seen in the word walls created by general education teachers. The *at* rime family contains all of the words that have different onsets and end in *at*.

Reaching the consolidated phase means that students are recognizing consonant blends (*bl-at, dr-at*) and vowel digraphs (*oo, ea*). Because of the manner in which the key vocabulary words are used to lead students into these phases, the full alphabetic phase and the consolidated alphabetic phase will most likely occur simultaneously with braille-reading students. In the consolidated alphabetic phase, the student learns to remember matches between sound units that may contain more than one letter, such as consonant blends or vowel blends. In this stage, the use of the onset and rime provide the opportunity for introduction of contractions and ending sounds for words, creation of word families, and expansion of reading vocabulary for braille readers.

Another way to increase the number of words recognized is to select key vocabulary words that have recognizable onset/rime spelling patterns. As an example, *fish* has the rime *ish* but *beautiful* does not have such an easily recognizable pattern. Both of these words could have been used in the partial alphabetic phase where initial consonants were the focus, but to move on to the ability to use onset/rime to decode new words involves more than simply being able to recognize consonants and vowels and put them together. Onset/rime patterns help students begin to be able to decode words by analogy. Thus, students analogize from *fish* to *dish*, as long as they are also able to recognize and say the initial sound for *d*.

With braille readers, both phases may extend a bit longer than with print readers, since there are more symbols to learn than just the letters of the alphabet. The important factor is to continue to motivate students to expand the number of words that they read, both as key vocabulary words and also as words that flow from their initial reading words and become part of their reading vocabulary.

SUGGESTIONS FOR USING KEY VOCABULARY WORDS IN THE STAGES OF PHONICS INSTRUCTION

Teachers may feel that using such an explicit but unscripted way of teaching phonics is a daunting task considering all of the contractions and symbols that need to be learned in braille. However, there are some things teachers can do to make the task easier for them and for their students and still relate what is being learned to meaningful words and stories.

The following are some suggestions that can help teachers use the key vocabulary and filler words a student knows to determine how to use them in phonics instruction as they move through the various stages. Note that not all key vocabulary or filler words will be equally useful for teaching phonics once the teacher begins working with students in the consolidated alphabetic phase.

Pre-Alphabetic Phase

- Work on the tactilely significant features of the key and filler words.
- Discuss how the word feels and learn the "language of touch" mentioned in Chapter 4.

Partial Alphabetic Phase

- Work on learning to identify the initial and tactilely distinct letters in some of the very important key vocabulary words the student has selected.
- Discuss the sound the letters make in the word and talk about other words that begin with that sound.
- The words chosen could represent activities, or foods, or possibly other students' names.
- Make a list of words that begin with a specific letter and let the student determine which of those words he or she might want to read or learn about.
- Sometimes a particular word may not already be in the student's vocabulary; thus it becomes an opportunity for concept development or vocabulary teaching to occur. The idea is to select some of these words as vocabulary words to incorporate into the student's reading vocabulary so the number of words that the student can read will continue expanding, with additional words also contributing to story development.
- Use the initial consonants of words the student already knows to provide for a large number of words to be added to the student's reading vocabulary.

Full Alphabetic Phase

- As students move toward completion of this phase, keep accurate records of the symbols the students have been introduced to and the ones they have mastered. A list of letters and contractions can be created for this recordkeeping purpose using a simple two-column format for checking introduction or mastery.

Consolidated Alphabetic Phase

- As students move further and further into this phase, teachers may want to start using a teaching kit similar to the Word PlayHouse, discussed in the next section.
- Have students create word families in braille and learn to recognize more words by learning their onset/rime patterns.
- Use words that are not within the student's experiential understanding to provide opportunities for discussion and possible field trips, thus expanding the student's vocabulary to include new words and concepts and enlarging his or her world.

Follow the student's lead. One student became enamored with the contraction *in*, which occurred in several of her key vocabulary words. At one point she asked her teacher if she could have a whole lot of *in* words. They spent several long lessons examining the various words that contain the *in* contraction. The student wanted to write stories in which all of the *in* words had to be included, which resulted in some silly sentences and much laughter. Having fun is the best way to learn!

As the student learns to read more and more key vocabulary and filler words, teachers will want to continue to record them in order to determine their utility in teaching phonics. Sidebar 8.1 provides a list of steps teachers can use for employing key vocabulary and filler words when teaching phonics. Teachers can separate the list into initial letter words or onset/rime words that can be used for teaching phonics and letter and contraction recognition. Teachers should also note which words have consonant blends (two or three consonants that make a distinct sound), digraphs (a single sound, or phoneme, represented by two letters), or which have various vowel sounds. Taking advantage of any teachable moment where the student notices or comments on a letter, letter combination, or contraction is important. Teachers will want to let the student know what it is that he or she is feeling, and then watch to see if the information sticks. Teachers do not need to insist that everything that is talked about is learned.

SIDEBAR 8.1

Steps in Using Key Vocabulary and Filler Words for Teaching Phonics and Phonemic Awareness

1. List all of the words the student has learned to recognize.
2. Analyze the words for initial consonant letters, or initial contractions. Make a list of these as the beginning sounds to work with.
3. Analyze the words for rimes. Some words will not have a rime, while other words may have one or even two possibilities.
4. Make note of any initial consonant letters or initial contractions that a student has commented on during lessons. These are good starting points for building skills with phonics and phonemic awareness.
5. Select the letter, contraction, or rime you are going to start with. (While most phonics skill builders start with initial sounds, braille students don't necessarily follow the typical patterns. So if a student is extremely interested in a contraction that is in the middle of the word, you can start with that. The important thing is to start somewhere.)
6. Ask the student if he or she can suggest other words that have that same sound. Be alert for sounds that are the same but that are spelled differently—for example, if the sound is /k/ and the letter you are working on is *c* as in /kat/. You may need to explain to a student that *cat* and *kitkat* are spelled differently. (See the Resources section for websites that provide information on the most common rimes.)
7. Create the list of words that the student will learn to read from the words suggested. Add other words that you know the student understands if the student doesn't suggest them.
8. Use the APH Word PlayHouse to help you in playing games with these sounds.

A general reading college-level textbook such as Vacca et al. (2012), Graves, Juel, Graves, and Dewitz (2011), or their most recent editions will provide the teacher with lists of phonics activities and the types of letter combinations to look for. The book *Reading Connections* (Kamei-Hannan & Ricci, 2015) also has many suggestions for phonics activities and games. Teachers who haven't already collaborated with the school district's reading specialist to learn about resources available in regular reading instruction may want to do so at this time, since there is so much available to help with teaching phonics.

USING THE WORD PLAYHOUSE TO TEACH PHONICS AND SPELLING SKILLS

The Word PlayHouse (available from the American Printing House for the Blind [APH]) is a kit that provides teachers with the opportunity to introduce and reinforce phonics and spelling skills related to students' key vocabulary words. The kit contains hundreds of tiles, referred to as cards, representing vowels, consonants, blends, diagraphs, word endings, and word families in large print with a braille overlay and a hook-and-loop material backing. A felt work board provides a working space for the student to manipulate letters and build words, word families, and new spelling and vocabulary words. Students enjoy manipulating the cards to create and read new words.

Setting Up the Kit for Use with Students

The Word PlayHouse kit comes with a large number of letter and letter combination cards, which can seem overwhelming to organize. However, it is not necessary to use all the cards at once; some cards with uncontracted forms of contractions and word family endings (rimes) may never be used at all. Initially, the teacher will only need the cards listed below. It is helpful to place each group of cards on a separate felt board and store it in the Word PlayHouse binder for easy access.

- the 26 consonant and vowel cards, with several duplicates of common letters
- consonant blends and digraphs that appear in the student's key words, such as *fl*, *sp*, *sh*, *th*, *ck*

The APH Word PlayHouse kit.

Courtesy of American Printing House for the Blind

- common rimes (word family endings) found in key vocabulary words that can be used to create rhyming words, such as *at, ide, eep, ack*
- contractions that appear in key vocabulary words
- capital signs created by the teacher using blank cards and adhesive braille labels that will be used for reading and spelling names

On the left side of the bifold felt work board, place the letters the student knows in alphabetical order at the top; place blends, word family endings, and contractions targeted for the current lesson below. Use one or more long thin strips from the Picture Maker: Wheatley Tactile Diagramming Kit (available from APH) or use Wikki Sticks to separate groups of cards, if desired, so individual cards are easier for the student to find during spelling activities. The right side of the work board is the work space for the teacher and student.

Teaching Tips

- Focus on onsets and rimes rather than sounding out words letter by letter. For example, if a student's key word is *bag* (for a bag of chips), segment the onset /b/ and the rime /ag/, rather than the three sounds /b/ /a/ /g/. Look for combinations of letters in longer key words that might be used to create new word families, such as the *ark* cluster in *Jordin Sparks* (a popular singer) or the *at* cluster in *tattoo*. The goal is to help students use letter combinations they already know to help them decode and spell new words.
- Include both decoding and encoding (spelling) activities. For example:
  - Decoding: make the *ag* rime on the right side of the work board. Substitute different onset consonants or consonant blends to create new words, asking the student to read each one, such as *rag, nag, tag, wag, flag.*
  - Encoding: make the *ag* rime on the right side of the work board and say a word in the *ag* family. Have the student find the initial consonant or consonant blend on the left side of the work board and place it in front of *ag.*
- After working with the Word PlayHouse cards, make written lists or word cards of words with the same rime (word families) for the student to read. Encourage the student to braille some or all of the words on the lists or cards.

GAMES AND ACTIVITIES FOR TEACHING PHONICS

Using the Word PlayHouse, there are many activities and games that teachers can implement with students to help teach them phonics. These are listed below. In addition, the Resources section includes several websites and books that have sources of games and materials for teaching phonics.

Scrambled Name

The teacher mixes up the letters in the student's name and has the student rearrange them in order. The teacher places a capital sign on the board to indicate where the name should begin. If the student has a long name or needs a slower pace, the teacher can make the name with only the first two letters missing. The teacher gradually increases the number of missing letters.

Riddles

On the right side of the board, the teacher makes a word family ending. The teacher gives the student a riddle and sees if he or she can complete the word that answers the riddle. For example:

1. Word family ending: *ake*
2. Riddle: teacher says, "I am thinking of something you eat on your birthday."
3. Response: student says, "cake," finds the *c* card, places it in front of *ake*, and reads the word.
4. Switch roles: the teacher gives the student a word family ending and asks him or her to think of a riddle.

Real or Nonsense?

The teacher selects a word family ending related to one of the student's key vocabulary words and places ten or more Word PlayHouse consonants or consonant blends that the student is familiar with in a small bag. Some should make a real word when added to the rime, and some should make a nonsense word.

The teacher has the student shake the bag, take out a letter, and place it before the rime on the work board. If it makes a real word, the student writes it by placing the letter in front of the rime. If it makes a nonsense word, the teacher writes it on a different line.

Read and compare the number of real and nonsense words.

Chunk Stacker

Chunk Stacker is a commercially available game that uses onsets and rimes. It is similar to the APH Word PlayHouse, except that it uses plastic tiles that can be stacked. Rather than stacking them, it is possible to affix braille to the tiles and create a game similar to the real or nonsense game just described. The teacher places ten or more onset tiles in a bag, asks the student to pick a tile from the bag, and uses a rime tile to place next to it to form a word. If the word makes sense,

Student using the Chunk Stacker game.

the student should try to use it in a sentence. If it doesn't, the student should simply say that it doesn't make sense.

Variation: the teacher can use a bag for the ten different rimes and select an onset that the student is familiar with. Draw a rime tile out of the bag and place it next to the onset. If the word is a real word, the student creates a sentence for it. If not, the student tells the teacher it doesn't make sense.

The next chapter will look at methods for applying and expanding student vocabulary through the use of trade books selected to correspond to student interest.

CHAPTER 9

Applying and Expanding the Student's Reading and Writing Vocabulary

Ms. Kendall's student, Jenny, asked to learn to read the word *tattoo*. Ms. Kendall asked her what she knew about tattoos, which was only that one of her cousins was going to get a tattoo and he mentioned that it would involve needles. Jenny wanted to know if the tattoo would hurt. Ms. Kendall took the opportunity to explain what a tattoo was, and compared it with some raised embroidery Jenny had on the jacket she was wearing. Ms. Kendall told Jenny that the tattoo was like the embroidery—it was a decoration—except that it was put on the skin, was smooth, and wouldn't go away once it was on. She also told Jenny that she didn't know if Jenny would be able to feel her cousin's tattoo once it had healed, like she can feel the embroidery. She explained that Jenny's cousin would probably go to a tattoo parlor to get the tattoo. She asked if Jenny knew what a "beauty parlor" was. Jenny did, and Ms. Kendall explained that the word *parlor* meant the place in which they provided the service of doing hair or doing tattoos. She asked Jenny if she knew what kind of tattoo her cousin was going to get. They talked about how it would probably hurt to have the needle put the ink into the skin. Jenny decided to ask her cousin more about getting a tattoo and to let Ms. Kendall know if she was able to feel it. While they were talking, Ms. Kendall brailled the word *tattoo* for Jenny to read. She made several word cards with *tattoo* on them, and gave them to Jenny to look at. Jenny was very excited to read the word, and couldn't wait to come back with more information about her cousin's tattoo for writing a story.

As teachers move through the various components of the I-M-ABLE approach, there will be times when they will find themselves discussing various topics of interest to the students, as demonstrated in the vignette about Jenny and the tattoo. These discussions help teachers ensure that their students' understanding of their world is accurate. These discussion times can also be used to expand students' language about their world, as Ms. Kendall did, particularly with the word *parlor*.

During their next lesson, Jenny told Ms. Kendall she knew a lot more about the tattoo her cousin was going to get and where he was going to get it. She wanted to write a story about it. Here is the story that she wrote with some probing questions from Ms. Kendall.

> Getting a **Tattoo**
> My cousin is going to get a **tattoo**.
> He wants to get a **tattoo** of an eagle.
> The **tattoo** will be on his left arm.
> He is going to the LA INK **tattoo parlor** to get his **tattoo**.
> He says that some people might think **tattoos** hurt, but that he is not a wimp.
> I would like to get a **tattoo**, too.

There were some new words and phrases in this story that Jenny had not had previous exposure to in writing. Ms. Kendall wrote the story in braille and had Jenny follow along. Then Jenny read the story again. Jenny was excited about her story and asked to read it by herself. When she paused, Ms. Kendall would supply the word or phrase. Some of the phrases that Jenny had not seen in braille included "is going to get," "will be," "on his left arm," and "LA INK," among others. Some of the words in the story involved braille wordsigns or groupsigns that Jenny had not yet learned. Ms. Kendall wrote these words down to include on word cards in the next lesson. For now, Jenny was happy that she had her story and could read most of it on her own.

Teachers need to keep in mind that they are not simply teaching reading, but they are also teaching language, especially to children who have been struggling readers and whose vocabularies can be very limited. Increasing a student's vocabulary in this way enlarges the student's understanding of the world while concurrently improving his or her ability to read about the world.

USING TRADE BOOKS

Another way to expand students' reading vocabularies is to have them read trade books on topics that interest them. It is important to make sure that these books are simple and easy to read. The Comprehensive Children's Book Center at the

School of Education, University of Wisconsin–Madison, publishes a comprehensive listing of children's books (both story books and trade books) on their website, which includes books based on rhyming, repetition, and so forth. (See the Resources section at the back of this book for more information about this and other sources of children's books.) Each book entry in the Comprehensive Children's Book Center listing includes the age range for which the book is most appropriate, so teachers can determine what books might fit their students' reading abilities by comparing that age range to the age level at which their students are currently reading. These books come from a variety of publishers.

Another means of finding trade books is simply to do an Internet search using the words "trade books on [topics] for beginning readers." Most of the websites that list trade books on a particular topic include a reading level by age. Many of these books may be available in the school library, but if not, the librarian may be able to order them so that the teacher can determine if they are appropriate for his or her student without having to purchase them. Teachers might also want to consult with a reading teacher in the school district to determine if they have access to any sources of trade books.

In addition, the American Printing House for the Blind (APH) has a website for early braille trade books (see the Resources section) that contains listings of books categorized by the contractions they contain, so teachers can predict which words students may have difficulty with and pre-teach those words in the context of getting ready to read the book. The APH early braille trade books are print books with transparent labels that contain the braille for each page. Teachers can purchase entire sets of these early trade books and braille labels through the APH Federal Quota System. APH is continually adding to these groups of trade books for purchase. Teachers can register to use this APH site with a student and can use the site to keep a running record of which contractions the student knows. The website will apply the information teachers provide about a student to the information that is contained about each book, and will indicate how many and which contractions the student would need to learn in order to be able to read the book independently.

Reading these short trade books is motivating to students who have not previously been successful in reading. Because the books contain both print and braille, students can take them home and read them to their parents, or read them aloud to anyone willing to listen, such as a paraeducator or another student who is a print reader, and the listener will be able to help the student if difficulty with a particular word is encountered.

TIPS FOR EXPLORING THE ENVIRONMENT FOR PRACTICAL USES OF BRAILLE

Another way to expand the students' language and reading and writing vocabulary is to create functional uses for braille in the environment. The following are some suggestions for ways to incorporate braille into daily activities. Depending on a student's writing ability, some of the braille writing may be done by the student, or it may be done by the teacher for those students who haven't yet mastered enough writing to use braille in the manner suggested. Teachers may have additional suggestions for their students.

- Explore the school offices to see if braille labels are in use. If they are, help the student read them. If braille labels are not in use, help the student (1) figure out what the labels should be, (2) help him or her write them in braille on labeling tape, and (3) stick them in the appropriate places.
- If the school has a daily newsletter that goes out with the cafeteria menu or other information in it, create a copy of this in braille for the student to read.
- Have the student write notes to friends and family. Notes can be birthday wishes, jokes, to-do lists, or play date invitations.
- Develop a braille recipe book that includes ingredients and directions.
- Make a list of the student's friends and their telephone numbers.
- Write out a shopping list in braille and read it while shopping, crossing off each item as it is put in the cart. (To cross off the items, put a sticker or piece of Wikki Stix on the braille, or simply rub out the first few letters of the item.)
- Label CDs, DVDs, or other similar items with braille.
- Make a book of jokes and their punch lines for the student to share with friends and family.
- Add braille to games such as UNO, Chutes and Ladders, or decks of cards, and teach students how to play.
- For a holiday or special meal, make place cards for each person in braille.
- Create braille song lyrics. Create a song book from the student's favorite songs.
- Keep score during games with braille score cards.
- Play games such as Bingo, Hangman, or a trivia game using cards written in braille.
- Prepare a menu for the day, week, or month using braille.
- Look for ways for students to use braille in jobs at home or in school. For example, at school, the child may need to put notices in certain teachers' mailboxes. Each mailbox can have a label with the teacher's name in braille.

- Conduct a simple survey. Braille a question containing a key vocabulary word (such as, "Do you like **pizza**?"), and help students tally the responses below the question. Make a tactile graph of the data.
- Create braille labels for a student's personal belongings and school materials such as binders, a lunchbox, and the like.
- Have the student give a presentation about braille to the class with the teacher of students with visual impairments. Braille classmates' names on index cards for the students to take home. (Don't forget the classroom teacher!)
- Teach classmates to write their names on the brailler. Demonstrate the finger positions for each letter, and have the students imitate them.
- Write gift tags for holiday presents. Have the student help pass out presents by reading the tags.
- Make a braille job chart for home, listing the chores down the left side and the days of the week across the top. Use stickers or stars to show when the chores are completed.

Sidebar 9.1 lists a number of functional uses of braille organized by the environments in which they might occur. The list, developed by teachers brainstorming different ways that braille could be used in these environments, contains items that might be beyond or below a student's current level (for example, choice making, which simply means that a student can make a choice between two things to eat or wear). Simply use the list to look for ideas to help students find and use more braille on a daily basis.

RECORDKEEPING

The teacher will want to keep track of the student's topics of interest in the student record book as a reference for finding trade books in these same areas. Keeping a list of trade books the student has read is also important, so that others know which books the student is capable of reading independently, or with assistance. The filler words that students learn as a result of reading these books can be added to their word lists, and word cards can be created for new words and phrases. The teacher can then include these words in the monthly probes.

The use of trade books is a good opportunity to practice fluent reading with prosody—correct inflection, intonation, or pitch—as discussed in the next chapter. Chapter 10 provides a discussion of techniques that can be used to help I-M-ABLE learners become fluent readers who demonstrate that they are reading with meaning.

SIDEBAR 9.1

Functional Uses of Braille in Different Environments

School

Reading directions, books
Taking notes, messages
Completing forms
Reading for information (lunch menus, announcements, schedules)
Locating items, materials
Completing assignments
Recording information
Locating rooms
Using maps
Making choices
Communicating
Labeling shelves, lockers
Reading combinations

Home

Labeling personal items (tapes, videos)
Telephone and address book
Writing and reading letters, notes, messages, recipes
Using a calendar
Labeling boxes, food containers
Marking clothing
Playing games, cards
Sending greeting cards
Taking messages
Reading magazines, newspapers
Writing, reading, sending mail
Managing money (maintaining savings or checking account)
Labeling appliances, equipment (remote control, VCR, and the like)
Labeling cabinets and drawers
Studying, reading, writing homework
Communicating

Community

Reading menus
Reading maps, bus schedules
Writing and reading shopping lists, directions
Using ATMs, elevators, restrooms

Work

Labeling items, equipment, machines
Organizing work, labeling file folders and file drawers
Taking and reading messages
Reading for information
Scheduling
Using checklists to complete work
Labeling personal items
Writing reminders
Handling mail
Maintaining work ID, timecard, and watch
Communicating

Source: Reprinted from Wormsley, D. P. (2000). *Braille literacy curriculum* (p. Section II, 6). Philadelphia: Towers Press.

CHAPTER 10

Helping Students Read Fluently

Although fluency has not yet been discussed in this practice guide as an instructional goal, fluency is important. *Fluency* is the ability to read text quickly, accurately, and with expression. It contributes to skilled reading and comprehension. Fluent reading relies on automatic word recognition, something I-M-ABLE strives to develop right from the beginning with the introduction of the key vocabulary words. Students feel successful when they are able to automatically recognize words that are meaningful to them. That success translates into motivation to continue learning to read.

I-M-ABLE presents strategies to help students learn to recognize words, read stories using those words, and write stories for reading. The approach emphasizes accuracy in word recognition (and subsequently in recognizing letters and contractions). The student's key vocabulary words are used for introducing word patterns and learning to recognize these patterns, such as onset/rime or consonant blends, for phonics and decoding instruction. As more and more words are introduced and students begin to read stories with both key vocabulary and filler words, accurate recognition is still expected. I-M-ABLE spends time on quick and accurate word recognition throughout. Fluent word recognition is often referred to as *automaticity,* involving both accuracy and speed (Kuhn, 2004).

The literature on fluency contains numerous suggestions for methods that will permit students to improve their reading fluency with the rationale that fluency has a positive impact on comprehension (Kuhn & Rasinski, 2011; Rasinski, 2009). In I-M-ABLE, comprehension as a goal is approached through ensuring that students understand the meaning of the words they are learning to read and assisting them with understanding the stories they write. For example, when using aspects of phonics such as onset/rime to add to a student's reading vocabulary, time is spent on making sure that these new words have meaning for the student.

To assess whether students are reading with fluency, teachers often use an assessment of correct words read per minute. With students who are learning to read using I-M-ABLE, one of the difficulties in making this assessment is that the students may have little in the way of connected text to read other than the stories that they have created, at least initially. Also, the number of correct words per minute may be small for these readers. However, incorporating some of the best practices in fluency instruction when students are learning to read the stories (connected text) they have written allows the students to develop their fluent reading at a pace that matches the words and stories they are reading. Trying to develop the reading fluency of these students apart from the meaningful materials they are learning to read might take more time than is necessary and will also take them away from their important work of learning to read words and stories that are meaningful to them.

STRATEGIES FOR DEVELOPING READING FLUENCY

Another aspect of fluency that contributes to skilled reading development (Kuhn, 2004) is *prosody*—how the written passage sounds when it is read with meaning, using pitch, stress, and appropriate phrasing. In addition to the strategies teachers are already using to develop accurate and quick word recognition, there are several strategies that teachers can incorporate into their I-M-ABLE lessons to help students who have not yet achieved the ability to read with expression. These strategies can be found in Kuhn and Rasinski (2011) who present Rasinski's (2009) four principles of fluency instruction:

1. modeling
2. support
3. focus on phrasing
4. reading continuous text

These four principles are described here and can be readily applied within the context of the I-M-ABLE approach.

Modeling

For Rasinski (2009), modeling emphasizes the importance of teachers reading aloud good children's literature, and setting aside daily times for teachers and other fluent readers to read aloud. This approach, however, may not work as well with students who are cognitively challenged and do not comprehend the material being read. Students who are not fluent readers may or may not have ideas of what fluent reading sounds like to use as a model for themselves when reading out loud. I-M-ABLE students often read out loud the stories that they have written using their key vocabulary words. Although they may have accurate and quick word identification, their initial reading of a story may fall within Levels 1 or 2 on the National Assessment of Educational Progress (NAEP) Oral Reading Fluency Scale (see Table 10.1), indicating that they are nonfluent. Reading with expression is tied to an understanding of the text being read; without that comprehension, children who listen to text being read may not link how the meaning influences the way the words are expressed. Not only are they listening a story that they don't understand, but, due to this lack of comprehension, they may not take away the model of fluency that might be expected. Therefore, this type of modeling of expressive reading may not carry over into students' own reading.

A better method for I-M-ABLE teachers to use is to model the fluent reading of stories that students do comprehend. Perhaps these are stories that students and

TABLE 10.1
National Assessment of Educational Progress Oral Reading Fluency Scale, Grade 4

Fluent	**Level 4**	Reads primarily in larger, meaningful phrase groups. Although some regressions, repetitions, and deviations from text may be present, these do not appear to detract from the overall structure of the story. Preservation of the author's syntax is consistent. Some or most of the story is read with expressive interpretation.
	Level 3	Reads primarily in three- or four-word phrase groups. Some small groupings may be present. However, the majority of phrasing seems appropriate and preserves the syntax of the author. Little or no expressive interpretation is present.
Nonfluent	**Level 2**	Reads primarily in two-word phrases with some three- or four-word groupings. Some word-by-word reading may be present. Word groupings may seem awkward and unrelated to larger context of sentence or passage.
	Level 1	Reads primarily word-by-word. Occasional two-word or three-word phrases may occur, but these are infrequent and they do not preserve meaningful syntax.

Source: U.S. Department of Education, Institute of Education Sciences, National Center for Education Statistics, National Assessment of Educational Progress. (2002). *Oral reading study: Oral reading fluency scale.* Washington, DC: Author. Retrieved from http://nces.ed.gov/nationsreportcard/studies/ors/scale.aspx

teachers have written, or a story that the teacher has written about the student and his or her interests. It might also be a children's book that the teacher and student have read together, with explanations of the meaning of the story, to ensure that the student understands it while having it read to him or her. Reading aloud a story that the student understands enables the student to hear how the expression changes as the meaning changes; another way of saying this is that it helps the student understand how the expression used in reading demonstrates the meaning of the phrases.

Teachers using I-M-ABLE create stories with their students right from the beginning of reading instruction. As each story is learned, the teacher can model the reading of the story with expression, even if it is only a few sentences in length. If the student does not follow the teacher's lead in trying to use expression, the teacher may have to explicitly call the student's attention to the prosody being used in the story. Modeling can be accompanied by support.

Support

After modeling the reading of a story with which the student is familiar, teachers may ask the student to read the story with them. This type of parallel reading is often referred to as *echo reading* or *paired reading*. The teacher reads along with the student to help the student when encountering something that isn't automatically recognized. The inflection and phrasing are modeled by the teacher during echo reading, just as the teacher did when reading the story solo to model the prosody. This provides support for fluency development while students are still learning to become accurate readers.

Choral reading is a form of echo reading where a number of students read the same passage together, with an emphasis on prosody. This may or may not be possible with I-M-ABLE students, depending on the type of setting for instruction.

Support can also be found in the form of audio recordings of the reading passage that a student can hear while at the same time reading the passage. These audio recordings may be teacher-made, or possibly professionally made, for stories that are typical children's stories. Practicing reading their braille version along with the recording to mimic the prosody will help students develop more fluent reading and feel more confident about their reading.

Focus on Phrasing

The third strategy teachers can use is to focus on the phrasing in a particular passage or paragraph. This includes demonstrating when to pause in reading, and when to combine all of the words together into a phrase for the purpose of expression. The result is something that sounds like talking—which is different from the monotone many beginning readers exhibit when reading. Teachers should model phrasing from time to time when a student is reading. The teacher can read the story first and provide the correct phrasing for a particular part of the story that may have previously been difficult for the student. When the student reads that portion of the story, the teacher can repeat it with the correct phrasing if the student has not phrased it correctly, or the teacher can praise the student for the correct phrasing if it was used.

Reading Continuous Text

The more a student reads, the more fluent his or her oral reading becomes. I-M-ABLE students will benefit from their teachers gradually increasing the amount of continuous (or connected) text that they read, and also providing text that becomes more and more challenging for the student. Kuhn and Rasinski (2011) indicated that research evidence shows that having students read connected texts and increasing the level of challenge in the materials that students read provides support for their becoming more fluent readers.

RECORDKEEPING

In order to monitor students' progress in attaining fluency, the teacher needs to measure not only the number of accurately read words per minute but also measure for prosody. Accurate words per minute can be assessed by noting how many words a student reads accurately within a five-minute time frame and then dividing that number by five. Teachers can then combine that measure of accurately read words per minute with an assessment of oral reading fluency such as that proposed by the NAEP Scale (see Table 10.1). This table also provides teachers with goals for reading fluency for their students in order to ensure that students are making progress.

CONCLUSION

This chapter covers fluency, the last component of I-M-ABLE, and is therefore the final chapter in this practice guide. As was mentioned at the beginning of the practice guide, the components of the approach are not designed to be used sequentially. Once a student has been exposed to tracking, for example, then tracking can be incorporated into each lesson. Once writing has been introduced, then each lesson can contain a segment involving writing. The Lesson Summary Sheet mentioned in Chapter 4 contains a listing of the components of the approach around which a particular lesson might be designed. A lesson can include multiple components, or only focus on one or two, depending on what the teacher feels is important for that particular lesson. Fluency is just one of those components, and can be the focus of a lesson as often as the teacher feels it is important.

It is my hope that the I-M-ABLE practice guide will provide teachers with the guidance needed to help their students who initially had difficulty learning braille to ultimately become readers. I also hope that teachers enjoy this process and share their experiences with others, either in writing or in workshops at state and local conferences. Finally, the fact that students who have visual impairments and additional disabilities can and do become readers is an important message to pass on to others in the field of blindness and visual impairment.

References

Anderson, R. C., Hiebert, E. H., Scott, J. A., & Wilkinson, I. A. G. (1985). *Becoming a nation of readers: The report of the Commission on Reading.* Washington, DC: U.S. Department of Education, The National Institute of Education.

Ashton-Warner, S. (1963). *Teacher.* New York: Simon and Schuster.

Bishop, V. E. (1991). Preschool visually impaired children: A demographic study. *Journal of Visual Impairment & Blindness, 85*(2), 69–74.

Charlson, K. (2010). *Drawing with your Perkins Brailler.* Watertown, MA: Perkins School for the Blind.

Ferrell, K. A., Shaw, A. R., & Deitz, S. J. (1998). Project PRISM: A longitudinal study of developmental patterns of children who are visually impaired (Final Report, CFDA 84.023C, Grant H023C10188). Greeley: University of Northern Colorado, Division of Special Education.

Gaskins, I. W., Ehri, L. C., Cress, C., O'Hara, C., & Donnelly, K. (1997). Procedures for word learning: Making discoveries about words. *The Reading Teacher, 50*(4), 312–327.

Graves, M. F., Juel, C., Graves, B. B., & Dewitz, P. (2011). *Teaching reading in the 21st century: Motivating all learners* (5th ed.). Boston: Pearson.

Hatton, D. D., Erickson, K. A., & Lee, D. B. (2010). Phonological awareness of young children with visual impairments. *Journal of Visual Impairment & Blindness, 104*(12), 743–752.

Kamei-Hannan, C., & Ricci, L. A. (2015). *Reading connections: Strategies for teaching students with visual impairments.* New York: AFB Press.

Kliewer, C. (2008). *Seeing all kids as readers: A new vision for literacy in the inclusive early childhood classroom.* Baltimore: Paul H. Brookes Publishing Co.

Koenig, A. J., & Holbrook, M. C. (2000). Ensuring high-quality instruction for students in braille literacy programs. *Journal of Visual Impairment & Blindness, 94*(11), 677–694.

Kuhn, M. (2004). Helping students become accurate, expressive readers: Fluency instruction for small groups. *The Reading Teacher, 58*(4), 338–344.

Kuhn, M. R., & Rasinski, T. (2011). Best practices in fluency instruction. In L. M. Morrow & L. B. Gambrell (Eds.), *Best practices in literacy instruction* (4th ed., pp. 276–294). New York: The Guilford Press.

Kusajima, T. (1974). *Visual reading and braille reading: An experimental investigation of the physiology and psychology of visual and tactual reading.* New York: American Foundation for the Blind.

Leu, D. J., & Kinzer, C. K. (1991). *Effective reading instruction K-8* (2nd ed.). New York: Merrill.

Lonigan, C. J., Anthony, J. L., Phillips, B. M., Purpura, D. J., Wilson, S. B., & McQueen, J. D. (2009). The nature of preschool phonological processing abilities and their relations to vocabulary, general cognitive abilities, and print knowledge. *Journal of Educational Psychology, 101*(2), 345–358.

Malloy, J. A., Marinak, B. A., & Gambrell, L. B. (2010). Introduction: We hope you dance: Creating a community of literate souls. In J. A. Malloy, B. A. Marinak, & L. B. Gambrell (Eds.), *Essential readings on motivation* (pp. 1–9). Newark, DE: International Reading Association.

Millar, S. (1997). *Reading by touch*. New York: Routledge.

Moustafa, M. (1997). *Beyond traditional phonics: Research discoveries and reading instruction*. Portsmouth, NH: Heinemann.

National Early Literacy Panel. (2008). *Developing early literacy; Report of the National Early Literacy Panel. Executive Summary*. Washington, DC: National Institute for Literacy. Retrieved from https://lincs.ed.gov/publications/pdf/NELPSummary.pdf

National Reading Panel. (2000). *Teaching children to read: An evidence-based assessment of the scientific research literature on reading and its implications for reading instruction*. Washington, DC: National Institute of Child Health and Human Development. Retrieved from www.nichd.nih.gov

Opitz, M. F., Rubin, D., & Erekson, J. A. (2011). *Reading diagnosis and improvement: Assessment and instruction* (6th ed.). Boston: Pearson.

Rasinski, T. V. (2009). Fluency for everyone: Incorporating fluency instruction in the classroom. In T. V. Rasinski (Ed.), *Essential readings on fluency* (pp. 17–20). Newark, DE: International Reading Association.

Senechal, M., LeFevre, J., Smith-Chant, B. L., & Colton, K. V. (2001). On refining theoretical models of emergent literacy: The role of empirical evidence. *Journal of School Psychology, 39*(5), 439–460.

Stratton, J. M., & Wright, S. (2010). *On the way to literacy: Early experiences for visually impaired children*. Louisville, KY: American Printing House for the Blind.

Strickland, D. S., & Schickendanz, J. A. (2009). *Learning about print in preschool: Working with letters, words, and beginning links with phonemic awareness* (2nd ed.). Newark, DE: International Reading Association.

Swenson, A. M. (2016). *Beginning with braille: Firsthand experiences with a balanced approach to literacy* (2nd ed.). New York: AFB Press.

U.S. Department of Education, Institute of Education Sciences, National Center for Education Statistics, National Assessment of Educational Progress. (2002). *Oral reading study: Oral reading fluency scale*. Washington, DC: Author. Retrieved from http://nces.ed.gov/nationsreportcard/studies/ors/scale.aspx

Vacca, J. L., Vacca, R. T., Gove, M. K., Burkey, L. C., Lenhart, L. A., & McKeon, C. A. (2012). *Reading and learning to read* (8th ed.). Boston: Pearson.

Wagner, R. K., Torgeson, J. K., & Rashotte, C. A. (1994). Development of reading-related phonological processing abilities: New evidence of bidirectional causality from a latent variable longitudinal study. *Developmental Psychology, 30*(1), 73–87.

Whitehurst, G. J., & Lonigan, C. J. (2003). Emergent literacy: Development from prereaders to readers. In S. B. Neuman & D. K. Dickinson (Eds.), *Handbook of early literacy research* (pp. 11–29). New York: The Guilford Press.

Wormsley, D. P. (2000). *Braille literacy curriculum*. Philadelphia: Towers Press.

Wormsley, D. P. (2004). *Braille literacy: A functional approach*. New York: AFB Press.

Wormsley, D. P. (2011). A theoretical rationale for using the Individualized Meaning-centered Approach to Braille Literacy Education with students who have mild to moderate cognitive disabilities. *Journal of Visual Impairment & Blindness, 105*(3), 145–156.

Wormsley, D. P., & D'Andrea, F. M. (Eds.). (1997). *Instructional strategies for braille literacy*. New York: AFB Press.

Wormsley, D. P., & McCarthy, T. (2013). *Trends in implementation of the I-M-ABLE approach*. Presentation at the Getting in Touch with Literacy Conference, Providence, RI.

APPENDIX
Blank Forms

Baseline Data Collection Form

Student's Name: _____

Date: _____

I. Attitude toward Reading and Braille
Motivation Questionnaire

Directions: "I am going to ask you some questions about how you feel about things and I want you to answer with the words 'awesome,' 'just okay,' or 'yucky.'" (You may feel it is necessary to discuss what these words mean in order for the student to use them correctly.)

Some things to keep in mind:
- Sometimes students like to perseverate on one or two of the answer words. Make sure they understand that they should be expressing what they really feel.
- Be aware that some students simply like the sounds of certain words and will say them just to hear the sound. For example, if the student is enamored with the word *awesome* used in the questionnaire, the teacher should substitute another, less appealing word for the student to use.
- A number of attempts answering some practice questions such as the following may be necessary.

Motivation Practice Questions
1. How do you feel about [a favorite food]? Is it awesome, just okay, or yucky?
2. How do you feel about [a food the student dislikes]? Is it awesome, just okay, or yucky?
3. How do you feel about [a best friend]? Is he/she awesome, just okay, or yucky?
4. How do you feel about [an activity that the student really doesn't like]? Is it awesome, just okay, or yucky?

- Continue with the practice questions until you are sure the student is answering with what he or she really feels. Try to find some neutral things or activities so that the student can also answer with "just okay."
- It is important to keep the tone of your voice neutral so that you don't lead the student to answer a particular question in a particular way.
- Once you are sure the student understands how to answer the questions, record his or her answers on the sheet below after each question. (There are 12 questions.)

Motivation Assessment Questionnaire

Student's Name: _____

Date of Administration: _____

1. How do you feel when someone reads a story to you? You can say "awesome," you can say "just okay," or you can say "yucky."

    Circle one: Awesome   Just Okay   Yucky

Diane P. Wormsley, *I-M-ABLE: Individualized Meaning-Centered Approach to Braille Literacy Education*, copyright © 2016, AFB Press, New York. This page may be copied for educational use only.

2. How do you feel about learning to read braille?

   Circle one: Awesome   Just Okay   Yucky

3. How do you feel about learning to write braille?

   Circle one: Awesome   Just Okay   Yucky

4. How do you feel when it is time for braille reading or writing class?

   Circle one: Awesome   Just Okay   Yucky

5. How do you feel when your teacher asks you to read braille?

   Circle one: Awesome   Just Okay   Yucky

6. How do you feel when your teacher asks you to write braille?

   Circle one: Awesome   Just Okay   Yucky

7. How do you feel about the stories you read in reading class?

   Circle one: Awesome   Just Okay   Yucky

8. How do you feel about reading instead of playing?

   Circle one: Awesome   Just Okay   Yucky

9. How do you feel when your teacher asks you questions about what you have read?

   Circle one: Awesome   Just Okay   Yucky

10. How do you feel when you read a story?

   Circle one: Awesome   Just Okay   Yucky

   Have you ever done that?

   Yes   No

11. How do you feel when you read a story to a friend or a child who is younger than you are?

   Circle one: Awesome   Just Okay   Yucky

   Have you ever done that?

   Yes   No

12. How do you feel about taking a reading test?

   Circle one: Awesome   Just Okay   Yucky

   Have you ever done that?

   Yes   No

Teacher's anecdotal notes on motivation:

(continued on next page)

Baseline Data Collection Form *(continued)*

II. Reading

Name Recognition: Three Names on a Line; Three Lines

- Use the child's name and two other names of similar length for this assessment. The additional names may be the names of friends or family members and should be similar in length to the student's name.
- Create a braille assessment sheet similar to the one in the example below. Use the child's name and two other different names in each of three rows, with three names per row and three spaces between each name. Mix up the order of the names from one line to the next.
- Give the following directions to the student: "Track across each line and find your name. You do not need to read the other names, just show me where your name is."
- As the student reads, refrain from providing any verbal or other assistance that might help the student identify his or her name, and do not indicate whether an answer is correct or incorrect. Spontaneous self-corrections may be counted as correct, but the last answer the student gives is the one scored (even if the first answer was right).
- Record the number of times out of three that the student is able to recognize his or her name.

Example

Assessment for *Jenny*. Distractors are *Brian* and *Mommy*.

Mommy	Brian	Jenny
Brian	Jenny	Mommy
Jenny	Mommy	Brian

Times student recognized his or her name: _____/3

Word Recognition

Does the student consistently recognize any braille words? Please list them here:

Letter Recognition

Using the following sequence of letters, prepare a braille assessment sheet using three double-spaced lines of letters with three braille spaces between each letter.

```
g  k  v  t  b  e  o  l  h
z  i  j  p  f  a  x  c  r
u  s  q  m  w  n  d  y
```

- Give the following directions to the student: "Here is a sheet of letters all mixed up. There are no contractions. Please read the letters to me. If you do not know a letter, just say, 'I don't know it' and continue with the next letter."

- Refrain from providing any verbal or other assistance that might help the student identify the letters, and do not indicate whether an answer is correct or incorrect. Spontaneous self-corrections may be counted as correct, but the last letter the student says for a particular symbol is the one scored (even if the first answer was right).
- Record the student's answers as follows using the rows of letters shown above:
  - Write a + above each letter the student reads correctly.
  - Write the letter the student says above each letter he or she reads incorrectly.
  - Circle the letters the student does not know.
  - Do not count a letter as correctly recognized if the student misreads another letter as that letter. (For example, if the student says *x* for *x* and then says *x* for *y*, do not count either as correct.)
  - Record the total number of letters the student can recognize. ____/**26**

Contraction Recognition

Does the student recognize any contractions in isolation or in words? Please list them here:

III. Writing

Name Writing

Can the student write his or her name independently and consistently using the Perkins Brailler?

Yes   No

Word Writing

Can the student write any other words independently and consistently using the Perkins Brailler?

Yes   No

If Yes is circled, please list these words below and indicate whether the student uses contracted braille when writing these words by placing parentheses around the contractions used.

Letter Writing

Can the student write any letters of the alphabet independently and consistently using a braillewriter?

Yes   No

(continued on next page)

Baseline Data Collection Form *(continued)*

If Yes is circled, please write the letters below:

IV. Phonemic Awareness/Phonics

If there are no results in the student's record for a test such as the Dynamic Indicators of Basic Early Literacy Skills (DIBELS) or the Texas Primary Reading Inventory (TPRI), teachers should work with their school district to have one of these tests administered to the student.

I-M-ABLE Fidelity of Implementation Checklist

1. Getting started and incorporating early literacy instruction
   - ☐ Exposes students to words and letters in braille
   - ☐ Models uses of braille reading and writing
   - ☐ Provides language for students to explain what is happening in the environment
   - ☐ Reads meaningful stories to students
   - ☐ Promotes concept development
   - ☐ Introduces and allows students to explore writing tools
   - ☐ Sets up a learning environment that is conducive to student learning
   - ☐ Involves others in teaching students

2. Selecting key words
   - ☐ Selects key vocabulary words with student input
   - Generates key words from:
     - ☐ Conversations with students
     - ☐ Observation of students
     - ☐ Consultation with other key people in students' lives (parents, other teachers, paraprofessionals, etc.); verifies with students
   - ☐ Responds to student selection of additional key words and incorporates student preferences in lessons
   - ☐ Uses filler words derived from need (e.g., story-making requires them)

3. Introducing key words
   - ☐ Ensures first several words are tactually distinct in length, features, etc.
   - ☐ Provides multiple copies of word cards for each word
   - ☐ Creates word cards correctly (lead-in lines as long as possible, proper spacing, correct braille contractions)
   - ☐ Tells students what words are; avoids testing
   - ☐ Demonstrates to students how to use the word cards (find lead-in line, use both hands together, track across the line—a space after the lead-in line indicates that a word will follow)
   - ☐ Introduces entire words; points out features of words
   - ☐ Provides ample repetition
   - ☐ Uses nonslip surface under cards
   - ☐ Assures proper furniture fit

4. Instruction in tracking
   - ☐ Incorporates key vocabulary words already introduced into initial instruction
   - ☐ Incorporates meaningful "story"
   - ☐ Ensures lines are at least double-spaced and of equal length
   - ☐ Ensures lead-in lines mirror those used in word cards; spaces before and after key vocabulary words

Diane P. Wormsley, *I-M-ABLE: Individualized Meaning-Centered Approach to Braille Literacy Education*, copyright © 2016, AFB Press, New York. This page may be copied for educational use only.

(continued on next page)

I-M-ABLE Fidelity of Implementation Checklist *(continued)*

- ☐ Demonstrates to students how to move their hands on the lines (both hands together like on the word cards)
- ☐ Demonstrates to students how to move from one line to the next (initially both hands go back over to the beginning of the line they are on and then down)
- ☐ Asks students to indicate in some fashion when they have found a word or words
- ☐ Uses nonslip surface under braille paper
- ☐ Ensures number of words per line matches student progress (initially no more than one per line, gradually increasing as competence in word recognition increases)
- ☐ Ties progression to more difficult tracking to students' capabilities (includes lines of varying lengths, tracking of sentences in stories of multiple lines, single spacing when appropriate)

5. Reinforcing word recognition through games
   - ☐ Reviews words to be used in games (words should be mastered by student)
   - ☐ Teaches students how to play the game (include a practice game)
   - ☐ Ensures others who might play games with students know how to play
   - ☐ Keeps records on which games students and others know how to play, and what words they are able to use when playing the game, as well as who students play the game with

6. Writing instruction
   - ☐ Uses backward chaining to assist students in learning to use the brailler
   - ☐ Incorporates writing into each section of the approach
   - ☐ Teaches correct finger position on keys (no curling under or lifting up of fingers)
   - ☐ Teaches students to look at what they have written after writing

7. Letter/contraction instruction
   - ☐ Uses initial letters from key vocabulary words to isolate for letter recognition
   - ☐ Creates letter cards for introducing the letters
   - ☐ Plays games with letters in isolation
   - ☐ Plays games with letters and words together
   - ☐ Uses contractions from key vocabulary words to isolate for contraction recognition
   - ☐ Explains what the contraction looks like and what letters it stands for; uses the letters to identify the contraction (for example, "this is the 't-h-e sign,' not the 'the' sign")
   - ☐ Introduces other words with the same letters or contractions for students to read

8. Phonics instruction
   - ☐ Is responsive to students (student interest in a particular letter/sound combination should generate acknowledgement on the part of the teacher); builds interests into subsequent lessons
   - ☐ Utilizes key vocabulary words in building phonics lessons

- ☐ Takes advantage of onset/rime patterns in key vocabulary words
- ☐ Takes advantage of grapheme/phoneme patterns in key words
- ☐ Makes new words from old; Word Wall activities (uses APH Word Playhouse when appropriate)
- ☐ Plays games with phonics; "tell me the real word" (Chunk Stacker games)

9. Creating stories with students
- ☐ Uses key vocabulary words to create (with the students) meaningful stories for them to read
- ☐ Uses filler words to create stories as they are needed
- ☐ Reads stories together with students until students can read the story independently
- ☐ Creates a folder for the stories students have generated and can read
- ☐ Provides opportunities for students to practice reading stories to others

10. Creating functional uses for braille
- ☐ Takes advantage of routines
- ☐ Takes advantage of holidays
- ☐ Creates uses related to the child's capabilities

11. Expanding students' reading/writing vocabulary
- ☐ Adds to reading/writing vocabulary from discussions
- ☐ Uses stories to create new words to read and write
- ☐ Uses phonics activities to create new words to read and write

12. Building fluency
- ☐ Incorporates daily practice in automaticity of word recognition
- ☐ Models prosody in reading stories
- ☐ Provides support for building fluency by using echo reading, tape recordings, and other appropriate supports such as repeated readings
- ☐ Focuses on correct phrasing for stories as appropriate
- ☐ Provides opportunities for students to read continuous text on a daily basis

13. Maintaining records
- ☐ Records daily lessons on Lesson Summary Sheet form (see Chapter 4)
- ☐ Maintains records of student mastery of words, and progress under each category above
- ☐ Helps students understand progress and feel successful
- ☐ Translates progress into performance on IEP goals

Form for Collecting Key Vocabulary Words			
Questions for Gathering Vocabulary	**Home Setting**	**School Setting**	**Community Setting**
Who are the significant people the student interacts with?			
Which words describe the student's daily routine?			
What are the student's hobbies, favorite things, and activities?			
Which words describe the student's work activities and chores?			

Source: Adapted with permission from Wormsley, D. P. (2000). *Braille literacy curriculum*. Philadelphia: Towers Press.

Diane P. Wormsley, *I-M-ABLE: Individualized Meaning-Centered Approach to Braille Literacy Education,* copyright © 2016, AFB Press, New York. This page may be copied for educational use only.

Form for Recording Words Learned, Practice Dates, and Mastery

Student's Name: _____

Word[a]	Intro Date	Practice Dates	Mastery Date	Sep Accuracy[b]	Oct Accuracy	Nov Accuracy	Dec Accuracy	Jan Accuracy	Feb Accuracy	Mar Accuracy

[a] K = Key; F = Filler
[b] + = Recognized; − = Missed

Diane P. Wormsley, *I-M-ABLE: Individualized Meaning-Centered Approach to Braille Literacy Education*, copyright © 2016, AFB Press, New York. This page may be copied for educational use only.

Lesson Summary Sheet

Directions for Using the Lesson Summary Sheet

This sheet is to be used for both planning and keeping records of what actually happened in the lesson.

Use one sheet per lesson. If more than one lesson takes place per day, use separate sheets for each.

<u>Complete</u> the top portion of the sheet with the student's name, date, and the individual who is working (or who is going to be working) with the student. Lesson start and end times should be filled in at the start and end of instruction. This will provide a running record of how much time is spent on lessons with the student.

Components

Underline the component or components that are planned for this lesson. Circle the ones actually worked on.

Plan for the Lesson

In this column, record the plan for the lesson, or, if providing guidance for another individual to work with the student, describe what he or she should plan to cover.

Instruction/Activities

This column should contain a description of what actually happened during the lesson. This may follow the plan closely or it might differ because a teachable moment presented an opportunity or because something extraneous occurred (a fire drill, for example, which can be both extraneous and a teachable moment).

Outcomes/Comments

In this column, record the outcomes of the lesson and include comments about child motivation, teacher motivation, or noteworthy happenings (such as things the student says, anecdotes, and the like).

Lesson Summary Sheet

Date: _____ Time started: _____

Student: _____ Time ended: _____

Instructor/other: _____

Components	Plan for the Lesson What do you plan to do?	Instruction/Activities What did you actually do?	Outcomes/ Comments
• Getting started • Key word introduction • Word recognition • Tracking • Reading stories • Writing stories • Phonics • Writing mechanics • Letter/contraction recognition • Vocabulary • Comprehension • Other: ____			

Diane P. Wormsley, *I-M-ABLE: Individualized Meaning-Centered Approach to Braille Literacy Education*, copyright © 2016, AFB Press, New York. This page may be copied for educational use only.

Mechanics of Using a Brailler: Assessment and Sequence of Skills

Recording Procedures:
I = Skill introduced
A = Skill achieved with assistance
M = Skill achieved with mastery

Skills	I	A	M
1. Identifies and uses the following parts of the brailler: embossing bar spacing keys backspacing key paper release levers paper feed knob embossing head lever line spacing key support bar feed roller left paper stop warning bell handle cover margin stop			
2. Operates brailler: Positions brailler correctly on work surface. Moves embossing head to correct positions. Rotates paper feed knob away from self. Pulls paper release levers all the way toward self. Holds paper against paper support with one hand and closes paper release with the other. Rolls paper into brailler until stopped by left paper stop. Depresses the line spacing key to lock paper position. Removes paper from the brailler. Leaves brailler in rest position when not in use (moves embossing head to the right as far as possible, leaves paper release lever open, and covers machine).			

Source: Reprinted from Wormsley, D. P., & D'Andrea, F. M. (Eds.). (1997). *Instructional strategies for braille literacy.* New York: AFB Press.

Diane P. Wormsley, *I-M-ABLE: Individualized Meaning-Centered Approach to Braille Literacy Education,* copyright © 2016, AFB Press, New York. This page may be copied for educational use only.

Resources

This section contains information that will help teachers locate resources for students who are learning to read using I-M-ABLE. Many of these resources are links to websites where information is readily available.

National Organizations (Blindness and Visual Impairment)

American Council of the Blind (ACB)
2200 Wilson Boulevard, Suite 650
Arlington, VA 22201-3354
(202) 467-5081; (800) 424-8666
Fax: (703) 465-5085
info@acb.org
www.acb.org

American Foundation for the Blind (AFB)
2 Penn Plaza, Suite 1102
New York, NY 10121
(212) 502-7600; (800) 232-5463
TDD: (212) 502-7662
Fax: (888) 545-8331
info@afb.org
www.afb.org

American Printing House for the Blind (APH)
1839 Frankfort Avenue
P.O. Box 6085
Louisville, KY 40206-0085
(502) 895-2405; (800) 223-1839
Fax: (502) 899-2284
info@aph.org
www.aph.org

Association for Education and Rehabilitation of the Blind and Visually Impaired (AER)
1703 N. Beauregard Street, Suite 440
Alexandria, VA 22311
(703) 671-4500; (877) 492-2708
Fax: (703) 671-6391
aer@aerbvi.org
http://aerbvi.org/

Council for Exceptional Children (CEC)
Division on Visual Impairments and Deafblindness (DVIB)
2900 Crystal Drive, Suite 1000
Arlington, VA 22202
(888) 232-7733
TTY: (866) 915-5000
Fax: (703) 264-9494
service@cec.sped.org
http://community.cec.sped.org
http://community.cec.sped.org/dvi/home

Hadley School for the Blind
700 Elm Street
Winnetka, IL 60093
(847) 446-8111; (800) 323-4238
TTY: (847) 441-8111
Fax: (847) 446-9820
info@hadley.edu
www.hadley.edu

National Braille Association
95 Allens Creek Road, Bldg. 1, Suite 202
Rochester, NY 14618
(585) 427-8260
Fax: (585) 427-0263
nbaoffice@nationalbraille.org
www.nationalbraille.org

National Federation of the Blind (NFB)
200 East Wells Street at Jernigan Place
Baltimore, MD 21230
(410) 659-9314
Fax: (410) 685-5653
nfb@nfb.org
https://nfb.org/

National Library Service for the Blind and Physically Handicapped (NLS)
Library of Congress
1291 Taylor Street, NW
Washington, DC 20542
(202) 707-5100; (800) 424-8567
TDD: (202) 707-0744
Fax: (202) 707-0712
nls@loc.gov
www.loc.gov/nls/

Perkins School for the Blind
175 North Beacon Street
Watertown, MA 02472
(617) 924-3434
info@perkins.org
www.perkins.org

Texas School for the Blind and Visually Impaired (TSBVI)
1100 W. 45th Street
Austin, TX 78756
(800) 872-5273
Fax: (512) 206-9453
www.tsbvi.edu

National/International Organizations (Literacy)

International Literacy Association (formerly International Reading Association)
P.O. Box 8139
Newark, DE 19714-8139
800 Barksdale Road
Newark, DE 19711-3204
(800) 336-7323 (US and Canada);
(302) 731-1600 (all other countries)
Fax: (302) 731-1057
customerservice@reading.org
www.literacyworldwide.org

Literacy Research Association
222 S. Westmonte Drive, Suite 101
Altamonte Springs, FL 32714
(407) 774-7880
Fax: (407) 774-6440
www.literacyresearchassociation.org

Sources of Braille Children's Books and Magazines

Encouraging children to read for pleasure, and thereby improving their skills, is a challenge for parents and teachers whether the medium is print or braille. Providing reading material that is interesting to the child is an excellent incentive.

This list provides sources for borrowing or purchasing braille and print/braille children's books and magazines in the United States. Please contact individual organizations for detailed information on products and prices.

Books

American Printing House for the Blind (APH)
1839 Frankfort Avenue
P.O. Box 6085
Louisville, KY 40206-0085
(502) 895-2405; (800) 223-1839
Fax: (502) 899-2284
info@aph.org
www.aph.org

Sells the *On the Way to Literacy* books, with print and braille and tactile illustrations. Also is a source for many other braille children's books, early learning materials, and the *Early Trade Books* series and its interactive website.

Braille Institute of America
741 North Vermont Avenue
Los Angeles, CA 90029
(323) 663-1111; (800) 272-4553
Fax: (323) 663-0867
la@brailleinstitute.org
www.brailleinstitute.org

Publishes *Expectations*, a free braille volume containing stories for elementary school–age children, plus some scratch-and-sniff pages. The book is sent out once a year around Christmastime. A summertime volume, *Brailleways*, is also available. Write to the Braille Institute of America to get on the mailing list. Other print/braille and braille children's books are available.

Braille International
3290 SE Slater Street
Stuart, FL 34997
(772) 286-8366; (800) 336-3142
Fax: (772) 286-8909
info@brailleintl.org

Offers the William T. Thomas bookstore with books for children (and adults). Books include the children's reference *State Books Series* with information about each U.S. state, plus Washington D.C. and Puerto Rico, and the *One to Grow On!* series of children's print/braille books with a read-along cassette. Other popular books and series, such as the *Baby-Sitters Club* books, are also available.

Braille Library and Transcribing Services
517 North Segoe Road, Suite 200
Madison, WI 53705
(608) 233-0222
Fax: (608) 233-0249
office.blts@tds.net
http://bltsinc.org

Braille books and print/braille books available for loan or purchase. All *American Girl* books available at less than print price. Catalog available.

Comprehensive Children's Book Center
School of Education
University of Wisconsin–Madison
401 Teacher Education
225 N. Mills Street
Madison, WI 53706
(608) 263-3720
ccbcinfo@education.wisc.edu
ccbc.education.wisc.edu

The center examines, studies, and maintains a research library of current, retrospective, and historical books published for children and young adults. Publishes a comprehensive listing of recommended children's books on a wide range of themes and topics.

Kenneth Jernigan Library for Blind Children
American Action Fund for Blind Children and Adults
18440 Oxnard Street
Tarzana, CA 91356
(818) 343-3219
JerniganLibrary@actionfund.org
www.actionfund.org

Maintains a lending library of print/braille books as well as braille books for K–12 grade reading and interest levels. Books are mailed to the child's home and also to schools. Contact the American Action Fund for Blind Children and Adults in writing for an application. Also offers a free braille calendar as well as a weekly newspaper for deaf-blind individuals. All services are free.

National Braille Press
88 St. Stephen Street
Boston, MA 02115
(617) 266-6160; (800) 548-7323 ext. 520
Fax: (617) 437-0456
orders@nbp.org
www.nbp.org

Offers a Children's Braille Book Club especially for preschool and primary grade children. The club offers access to popular picture books with the insertion of clear plastic sheets that contain the braille translation. There is no fee to join the club, and you can buy as few or as many books as you wish.

National Library Service for the Blind and Physically Handicapped (NLS)
Library of Congress
1291 Taylor Street, NW
Washington, DC 20542
(202) 707-5100; (800) 424-8567
TDD: (202) 707-0744
Fax: (202) 707-0712
nls@loc.gov
www.loc.gov/nls/

Offers a wide variety of braille books on loan. Call your regional library or NLS for more information and an application. NLS has also compiled a directory, available free of charge in large print and braille formats, which gives the names of volunteer groups and individuals who transcribe and record books and other reading materials for blind readers. The listing is alphabetical by state.

Seedlings Braille Books for Children
P.O. Box 51924
Livonia, MI 48151-5924
(734) 427-8552; (800) 777-8552
info@seedlings.org
www.seedlings.org

Offers more than 650 titles at reasonable prices for braille readers up to age 14. Choose from print and braille preschool picture board books, beginning reader print and braille books, and braille-only chapter books through middle school reading level on many different topics including a variety of books in uncontracted braille. Seedlings also offers free *World Book Encyclopedia* articles in braille through The Rose Project.

Magazines

American Printing House for the Blind (APH)
1839 Frankfort Avenue
P.O. Box 6085
Louisville, KY 40206-0085

(502) 895-2405; (800) 223-1839
Fax: (502) 899-2284
info@aph.org
www.aph.org

Offers several publications available from September through May. *My Weekly Reader* is a scholastic journal for grades 2–6 that focuses on current events. *Know Your World Extra!* is geared to youngsters ages 10–16 who have reading difficulties. Others also available: *Current Events* and *Current Science*. For subscription information, write or call the American Printing House for the Blind.

Christian Record Services for the Blind
4444 South 52nd Street
Lincoln, NE 68516
(402) 488-0981
Fax: (402) 488-7582
nfo@christianrecord.org
www.christianrecord.org

Makes two quarterly braille magazines available free of charge. *Children's Friend* has stories for children and *Young and Alive,* a publication for young adults, contains adventure fiction and devotional articles.

Lutheran Library for the Blind
Lutheran Braille Workers
13471 California Street
Yucaipa, CA 92399
(909) 795-8970; (800) 215-2455
LLB@lbwinc.org
www.lbwinc.org/library

Offers four free publications. *Happy Times* is a monthly magazine of religious articles and fiction for children ages 6–8. *My Pleasure*, also available monthly, contains stories for children ages 9–12. *My Devotions* has a month's worth of daily devotionals for children ages 8–13. *Teen Time* is published eight times a year and contains religious stories for young adults.

National Library Service for the Blind and Physically Handicapped (NLS)
Library of Congress
1291 Taylor Street, NW
Washington, DC 20542
(202) 707-5100; (800) 424-8567
TDD: (202) 707-0744
Fax: (202) 707-0712
nls@loc.gov
www.loc.gov/nls/

Offers a number of magazines for children of all ages, including: *Boys' Life, Muse, Spider: The Magazine for Children, Stone Soup,* and *Seventeen*. Subscriptions are free of charge and are available through your cooperating NLS regional library.

Sources of High-Interest Low-Vocabulary Books (Hi-Lo Books)

The high-interest, low-vocabulary books produced by the companies listed here are available in print, with the exception of those from the American Printing House for the Blind, which are available in large print or braille. Teachers may want to search for books on topics that they know are of interest to their specific students and then search the Louis database maintained by APH or the catalogs of braille publishers listed in the previous sections to see if these books are already available in braille. If books are not already available in braille, it is possible to have them brailled by one of the various transcriber organizations, which can be located through the National Library Service (see the section on National Organizations), or the *AFB Directory of Services*.

Academic Communication Associates
P.O. Box 4279
Oceanside, CA 92052-4279
(760) 722-9593; (888) 758-9558
www.acadcom.com

Academic Therapy Publications (High Noon Books)
20 Leveroni Court
Novato, CA 94949-5746
(800) 422-7249
Fax: (888) 287-9975
www.highnoonbooks.com

American Printing House for the Blind (APH)
1839 Frankfort Avenue
P.O. Box 6085
Louisville, KY 40206-0085
(502) 895-2405; (800) 223-1839
Fax: (502) 899-2284
info@aph.org
www.aph.org

Capstone Press
1710 Roe Crest Drive
North Mankato, MN 56003
(800) 747-4992
Fax: (888) 262-0705
www.capstonepub.com

Houghton Mifflin Harcourt Pre-K–12
9400 Southpark Center Loop
Orlando, FL 32819
(407) 345-2000; (800) 225-5425
www.hmhco.com/classroom

Lakeshore Learning Materials
2695 E. Dominguez Street
Carson, CA 90895
(310) 537-8600; (800) 778-4456
Fax: (800) 537-5403
lakeshore@lakeshorelearning.com
www.lakeshorelearning.com

Lerner Publishing Group
1251 Washington Avenue North
Minneapolis, MN 55401
(800) 328-4929
Fax: (800) 332-1132
info@lernerbooks.com
www.lernerbooks.com

New Readers Press
104 Marcellus Street
Syracuse, NY 13204
(800) 448-8878
Fax: (866) 894-2100
www.newreaderspress.com

Perfection Learning
1000 North Second Avenue
P.O. Box 500
Logan, IA 51546-0500
(800) 831-4190
Fax: (800) 543-2745
orders@perfectionlearning.com
www.perfectionlearning.com

Saddleback Educational Publishing
3120-A Pullman St.
Costa Mesa, CA 92626
(714) 640-5200; (800) 637-8715
Fax: (888) 734-4010
www.sdlback.com

Predictable and Trade Books
Predictable Books

Educational Resource Center
library.bridgew.edu/maxweb/pdf/predictable.pdf

Handy Handouts: Learning through Predictable Books
www.superduperinc.com/handouts/pdf/278_PredictableBooks.pdf

Predictable Patterns Books
literacy.kent.edu/Oasis/Pubs/patterns.html

Types of Predictable Books with Suggestions
pabook.libraries.psu.edu/familylit/LessonPlan/rover/ParentEducation/Types_of_Predictable_Books_Charts.pdf

University of Wisconsin–Oshkosh
www.uwosh.edu/library/emc/bibliographies/emc-bibliographies/predictable-books

Trade Books

Comprehensive Children's Book Center, School of Education, University of Wisconsin–Madison
http://ccbc.education.wisc.edu/books/bibBio.asp

Early Braille Trade Books, American Printing House for the Blind
https://tech.aph.org/ebt/

Phonics and Word Recognition Resources for Teaching

Essential Word Reading Lists
www.wilkinsfarago.com.au/PDFs/Reading_Spelling_Lists.pdf

Most Common Rimes
www.cram.com/flashcards/37-most-common-rimes-255531

Reading Rockets
www.readingrockets.org/strategies/onset_rime

Spectronics
www.spectronics.com.au/article/onset-rime-word-families

Assessments

Dynamic Indicators of Basic Early Literacy Skills (DIBELS)
https://dibels.uoregon.edu/

Texas Primary Reading Inventory (TPRI)
https://www.tpri.org/index.html

Sources of Products

This section lists some of the sources for the products mentioned in this book.

American Printing House for the Blind (APH)
1839 Frankfort Avenue
P.O. Box 6085
Louisville, KY 40206-0085
(502) 895-2405; (800) 223-1839
Fax: (502) 899-2284
info@aph.org
www.aph.org

Manufactures and distributes a wide assortment of educational and daily living products including the Swing Cell, Pop-A-Cell, slates and styli, Perkins Brailler, Swail Dot Inverter, Peg slate, Big Cell, GlowDice, braille calendars, Brailon, and braille paper. Manufactures a wide assortment of educational and daily living products; modifies and develops computer-access equipment and software; maintains an educational research and development program concerned with educational methods and educational aids; and provides a reference catalog service for volunteer-produced textbooks in all media for students who are visually impaired and for information about other sources of related materials.

Exceptional Teaching
P.O. Box 2330
Livermore, CA 94550
(925) 961-9200; (800) 549-6999
Fax: (925) 961-9201
info@exceptionalteaching.com
www.exceptionalteaching.com

Manufactures and distributes a wide variety of educational materials and curricula, especially for children with special needs, including tactile marking dots, Wikki Stix, shelf liner, and rubber mats for braillers.

FlagHouse
601 FlagHouse Drive
Hasbrouck Heights, NJ 07604-3116
(201) 288-7600; (800) 793-7900
info@flaghouse.com
www.flaghouse.com

Sells a variety of products, including Dycem nonslip material.

HumanWare
1 UPS Way
P.O. Box 800
Champlain, NY 12919
(800) 722-3393
Fax: (888) 871-4828
info@humanware.com
www.humanware.com

Distributes a variety of products including electronic notetakers and the Mountbatten brailler.

Perkins
175 North Beacon Street
Watertown, MA 02472
(617) 924-3434
info@perkins.org
www.Perkins.org

Manufactures and distributes the Perkins Braillers, including one-handed and other versions, slates and styli, and braille paper and extended keys for one-handed brailling.

Index

Note: The italicized letters *f*, *p*, and *t* following page numbers refer to forms or figures, photographs, and tables, respectively.

A

academic reading stage, 11*t*
activities
    daily, incorporating braille into, 114–115, 116*s*
    favorite of student, basing key vocabulary words on, 36
    incorporating into classroom practice time, 30
    phonics instruction using, 108–110
    using with key vocabulary stories, 93–97
advanced reading stage, 11*t*
American Printing House for the Blind (APH), 22, 113
analytic (whole-to-part) approach to phonics instruction, 98
Ashton-Warner, Sylvia, 1, 35
assessments
    collecting baseline data, 13–19
    collecting information about student's interests, 19–20
    determining what student already knows, 29
    intellectual climate, 21–26
    physical environment, 29
    social/emotional environment, 26–29
    student's learning environment, 20–29
attitude toward reading and braille, collecting information about, 14*f*–15*f*
audio recordings, 94, 120
automaticity, 117
availability of media, 24–25

B

background experience, 4–5, 22
backward chaining, 80
Baseline Data Collection Form, 13–18, 14*f*–18*f*, 19
beginning reading stage, 10–11, 11*t*
books
    applying and expanding vocabulary using, 112–113
    predictable, 23, 23*s*
    trade books, 112–113
braille. *See also* braillers; multiple lines of braille, tracking across; writing
    attitude toward, collecting information about, 14*f*–15*f*
    contracted, 39–41, 40*s*
    incorporating into daily activities, 114–115, 116*s*
    labels in, 114
    multiple lines of, 52
    opportunities to experience, 24–25, 26*s*, 27*s*
    tactile differences between words, 38–39
    writing in, 68
braille notetakers. *See* notetakers, electronic
braillers. *See also names of specific braillers*; writing
    brailling tracking stories, 82–83
    drawing using, 83–84
    hand and finger positions on, 85*p*
    loading and removing paper from, 81*f*
    mechanics of using, 75, 76*f*
    motivation to use, 79
    parts of, 85*f*
    types of, 75, 77*p*, 78*p*
    using with key vocabulary stories, 88, 91, 95–96, 97

C

capital dots, 52, 88, 90, 94, 96
capital letters, 90, 94
capital signs, 108–109
cards, for key vocabulary words or phrases, 43–45
    creating, 44*s*
    sharing, 62
choral reading, 120
classrooms, physical size of, 29
collaborative stories. *See* key vocabulary stories
collaborative writing, 84–86
communication, with classroom staff and parents, 30–31
components of I-M-ABLE, 8
Comprehensive Children's Book Center, 112–113
conceptual understanding, assessing, 22–23
consolidated alphabet phase, in phonics instruction, 103, 105–106
consonant blends, 103, 107, 108

continuous text, 121
contractions
 in key vocabulary words, 39–41, 40s
 learning in partial alphabetic phase, 102
 recognition assessment, 17f

D

daily activities, incorporating braille into, 114–115, 116s
diagnostic teaching, 5
DIBELS (Dynamic Indicators of Basic Early Literacy Skills), 18f, 19
dot density, 43
drawings
 brailling of, 82–83
 tactile, adding to books, 24
Dynamic Indicators of Basic Early Literacy Skills (DIBELS), 18f, 19, 131f

E

early literacy instruction
 frequency of instruction, 29–30
 getting started, 31
 involving others in, 30–31
echo reading, 120
electronic notetakers, 75, 95–96
emergent reading stage, 10–11, 11t
emotional environment. *See* social/emotional environment
emotionally laden words. *See* key vocabulary words or phrases
engagement in reading, 6
evaluations. *See* assessments
expectations of teachers for students, 21–22
experiences of students
 relating to current learning material, 4–5
 writing about, 88–89

F

Federal Quota System, 113
Fidelity of Implementation Checklist, 31, 32f–34f
finger numbing, 55–57
finger positioning
 when tracking, 46–47
 when writing, 78–80
fluency
 assessing, 118
 importance of, 117
 principles of instruction in, 118
 recordkeeping, 121
 strategies for developing, 118–121
Form for Collecting Key Vocabulary Words, 36, 38f
Form for Recording Words Learned, Practice Dates and Mastery, 55, 56f, 64–65
foundational skills supporting process of learning to read, 11–12
frequency of instruction, 29–30
full alphabetic phase, in phonics instruction, 102–103, 105
functional uses of braille in environment, 114–115, 116s

G

games, phonics
 Chunk Stacker, 109–110, 110p
 Real or Nonsense?, 109
 riddles, 109
 Scrambled Name, 109
games, word recognition
 Concentration game, 60
 Fishpond game, 62
 Mad Libs game, 61
 Monster Munch game, 62, 63p
 Pick the Word That Makes Sense game, 61
 sharing word cards, 62
 sorting games, 60
 talking card reader activity, 62–64, 64p
 tips for playing, 59–60
 using with key vocabulary stories, 93–97
 Which Two are the Same? game, 61
guiding principles of I-M-ABLE, 6–7

I

I-M-ABLE (Individualized Meaning-Centered Approach to Braille Literacy Education)
 components of, 8
 difference from traditional approaches, 2–3
 guiding principles of, 6–7
 how to use practice guide for, 7–9
 naming of approach, 1
I-M-ABLE Student Record Book, 19, 21s
independence, providing opportunities for, 31
individualization, 6–7
Individualized Meaning-Centered Approach to Braille Literacy Education. *See* I-M-ABLE
intellectual climate, 20, 21–26
interests of students
 basing key vocabulary words on, 35–37
 collecting information about, 19–20

K

key vocabulary stories
 audio recorded stories, 94
 cut-apart stories, 94
 first collaborative stories, 87–91

games and activities with, 93–97
helping students write own stories, 95–97
incorporating technology with, 94–95
language experience stories, 88–89
magnetic word board use with, 94, 95p
making books out of, 93
modeling of writing, 96–97
overview, 87
punctuation in, 90
reading stories, 91–93
recordkeeping, 97
samples of, 91–93
using real objects, 89–90
writing sentences, 94
key vocabulary words or phrases, 1, 35–41. *See also* key vocabulary stories; key vocabulary words, phonics instruction using
building and analyzing list of, 37–39
cards for, 43–45, 44s, 62
collecting and identifying, 35–37, 37s, 38f
contractions, 39–41
creating tracking stories using, 69–72
emphasizing differences between, 51–52
friends of students, basing words on, 36
identification of differences between, 53
introducing first key word, 45–46
introducing second key vocabulary word, 51–52
language of touch to describe, 49–51
lessons and games for reinforcing recognition of, 59–64
mastery of, 54–55
onset/rime spelling patterns in, 103
pace of lessons using, 55
people, favorite of student, basing words on, 36
recordkeeping of lessons using, 64–68
reviewing, 58–59
tactile differences between, 38–39
tracking, 46–49, 52
word recognition, 53–54
writing of, 44s, 68
key vocabulary words, phonics instruction using
games and activities for, 108–110
stages of phonics instruction, 104–106
steps in, 106s
using Word PlayHouse, 107–108

L

labels, braille, 114
language experience stories, 88–89
language of touch, 49–51
language-rich environments, 26s
lead-in/lead-out lines, 43, 47–48, 52, 70, 82
learning environment, 20–29
Lesson Summary Sheet, 65–67, 66f–67f
letter recognition assessment, 16f–17f
letter writing assessment, 17f
logographic phase, in phonics instruction. *See* pre-alphabetic phase, in phonics instruction

M

magnetic word board, 94, 95p
meaningful stories, 24–26
Mechanics of Using a Brailler form, 75, 76f, 84
media, availability of, 24–25
meeting with staff, to explain approach, 30
modeling, of reading, 119–120
monthly probes, 64–65
motivation
collecting information about, 13, 14f–15f, 18
importance of, 6
to use braillers, 79
Mountbatten brailler, 68, 75, 78p, 83
multiple lines of braille, tracking across, 52
and moving to next line, 72–74
reading stories, 74
tracking stories, 69–74, 71s–72s

N

NAEP (National Assessment of Educational Progress) Oral Reading Fluency Scale, 119, 119t
name recognition assessment, 16f
name writing assessment, 17f
National Assessment of Educational Progress (NAEP) Oral Reading Fluency Scale, 119, 119t
notetakers, electronic, 75, 95–96
numbing of fingers, 55–57

O

onsets, 103, 105, 108, 109–110, 117
oral language and concept development, 12

P

pace of lessons, 55
paired reading, 120
parallel reading, 120
parents of students
   celebration of student's success by, 28–29
   communication with, 30–31
   identifying key vocabulary words with help of, 36
   social/emotional climate assessment and, 27–29
partial alphabetic phase, in phonics instruction, 99–102, 104
Perkins Brailler, 68, 77p
   drawing using, 84
   fingering using, 78–81
   hand and finger positions on, 85p
   key configuration of, 79f
   light-touch, 77p
   models of, 75
Perkins SMART Brailler, 68, 75, 77p, 83
personalization, 6–7
phonemes, 12
phonemic awareness
   definition of, 12
   skills assessment, 18–19, 18f
phonics instruction
   analytic (or whole-to-part) approach to, 98
   games and activities for, 108–110
   phases in, 99–103
   resources for, 147
   stages of, 104–106
   using Word PlayHouse, 107–108
phonological processing, components of
   phonological awareness, 12
   phonological memory, 12
   phonological sensitivity, 12
   skills assessment, 18–19
phrasing, focusing on, 120–121
physical environment, 20, 29
pictures, 22
Pop-A-Cell, 100–102, 101p
practical uses of braille in environment, 114–115
practice time in classroom, incorporating activities into, 30
pre-alphabetic phase, in phonics instruction, 99, 104
predictable books, 23, 23s
prosody, 118, 120, 121
punctuation, 90

R

reading. *See also* books; braille; early literacy instruction; key vocabulary stories; key vocabulary words or phrases; phonics instruction; tracking
   assessment of, 16f–17f
   of key vocabulary stories, 91–93
   fluency in, 117, 118–121
   modeling of, 119–120
   motivation for, 6, 13, 14f–15f, 18
   stages of development, 10–11, 11t
recording lessons, 67–68
recordkeeping, 64–68
   key vocabulary stories, 98
   documenting tracking skills, 72
   fluency, 121
   vocabulary, applying and expanding, 115–117
   writing lessons, 84
responsiveness to students, 2–3
rimes, 103, 105, 106s, 117
   in games and activities, 109–110
   most common, 147
   in Word PlayHouse kit, 107–108

S

schema, 4–5
scrubbing of braille characters, 43, 48–49
sentences, writing, 94
sharing word cards, 62
SimBraille, 42
SMART Brailler, Perkins, 68, 75, 77p, 83
smooth tracking, 43, 45, 47–48, 74
social/emotional environment, 20, 26–29
space for teaching, 29
spelling skills, 107–108
staff
   celebration of student's success by, 28–29
   communication with, 30–31
   meeting with to explain approach, 30
stages of reading development, 10–11, 11t
Steps for Loading and Removing Paper from a Brailler form, 81f
stories. *See also* key vocabulary stories; tracking stories
   created by teachers, 23
Student Record Book, 19, 21s
success in reading
   celebration of, 28–29
   effects of, 7
support for fluency, 120
Swing Cell, 49, 100, 101p, 102

T

tactile cue phase, 99
tactile differences, between key vocabulary words, 38–39

Index

Talking Card Reader, 30, 62, 64*p*, 94
teachable moments, 57–58
teachers
    celebration of student's success by, 28–29
    expectations of, for students, 21–22
    stories created by, 23
technology, incorporating with key vocabulary stories, 94–95
Texas Primary Reading Inventory (TPRI), 18–19, 18*f*
touch, language of, 49–51
TPRI (Texas Primary Reading Inventory), 18–19, 18*f*
tracking, 46–49. *See also* multiple lines of braille, tracking across; tracking stories
    documenting tracking skills, 72
    finger position, 46–47
    key vocabulary words or phrases, 46–49
    nonslip surface for, 46
    smooth tracking, 43, 45, 47–48, 74
    whole word, focus on when, 48–49
tracking stories, 71*s*–72*s*
    brailling, 82–83
    creating using key vocabulary words, 69–72
    examples of, 70, 72
    using to teach tracking across a line and move to next, 72–74
trade books, 112–113

V

video recording lessons, 67–68
visual cue phase, in phonics instruction. *See* pre-alphabetic phase, in phonics instruction
vocabulary, applying and expanding, 111–116. *See also* key vocabulary words or phrases
    by incorporating braille into daily activities, 114–115, 116*s*
    recordkeeping, 115–117
    using trade books, 112–113
vowel digraphs, 103, 107

W

whole-to-part (analytic) approach to phonics instruction, 98
word board. *See* magnetic word board
Word PlayHouse, 107–108, 107*p*
word recognition assessment, 16*f*
    testing for, 54
word writing assessment, 17*f*
writing, 44*s*, 75–86. *See also* braillers; key vocabulary stories
    assessment of, 17*f*–18*f*
    collaboration on, 84–86
    fingering, 78–80
    as fun activity, 77
    incorporating into lessons, 81–82
    of key vocabulary words or phrases, 68
    motivation to write, 79
    reading of student's own, 83–84
    recordkeeping of lessons, 84
    of tracking stories, 82–83

About the Author

Diane P. Wormsley, Ph.D., has worked for over 40 years with adults and children of all ages with visual impairments, including those with additional disabilities. Dr. Wormsley is retired from her position as Brenda Brodie Endowed Chair and Professor, Special Education at North Carolina Central University; she is also a past program director and associate professor of the professional preparation program at the Pennsylvania College of Optometry (now Salus University). She is the author of *Braille Literacy: A Functional Approach* and *Braille Literacy Curriculum* and co-editor of *Instructional Strategies for Braille Literacy*. Dr. Wormsley is a former Editor-in-Chief of the *Journal of Visual Impairment & Blindness (JVIB)*, has published numerous articles on teaching students with disabilities, the ABC Braille Study, and braille literacy, and has presented on those topics at conferences around the world.

Dr. Wormsley began her teaching career at the New York State School for the Blind and also taught in Australia and Papua New Guinea. It was while teaching in Papua New Guinea that she came across the book by Silvia Ashton-Warner that was the impetus for the development of I-M-ABLE.

Dr. Wormsley is the recipient of the Alan J. Koenig Research in Literacy Award and the Holbrook-Humphries Award from Getting in Touch with Literacy, as well as the Mary K. Bauman Award and the C. Warren Bledsoe Award for *Instructional Strategies for Braille Literacy,* both from the Association for Education and Rehabilitation of the Blind and Visually Impaired. Dr. Wormsley continues her work in the field of blindness and visual impairment as an education consultant and as Associate Editor of *JVIB*.

CPSIA information can be obtained
at www.ICGtesting.com
Printed in the USA
LVOW05s0614230816
501409LV00003B/11/P